FAILURE
is not
the
END

...It's Your Stepping Stone to Success

FAILURE
is not the END

...It's Your Stepping Stone to Success

DENNIS LEONARD

FAILURE IS NOT THE END ...It's Your Stepping Stone to Success

Dennis Leonard
9495 East Florida Avenue
Denver, CO 80247
(303) 369-8514
www.dennisleonardministries.com

ISBN 1-880809-92-3
Printed in the United States of America
© 2004 by Dennis Leonard

Legacy Publishers International
1301 South Clinton Street
Denver, CO 80247
www.legacypublishersinternational.com

Cover design by: Tony Laidig - www.thirstydirt.com

1 2 3 4 5 6 7 8 9 10 / 09 08 07 06 05 04

CONTENTS

CONTENTS CONTINUED

INTRODUCTION

So the sons of Israel wept for Moses in the plains of Moab thirty days; then the days of weeping and mourning for Moses came to an end (Deut. 34:8).

Now it came about after the death of Moses the servant of the LORD that the LORD spoke to Joshua the son of Nun, Moses' servant, saying, "Moses My servant is dead; now therefore arise, cross this Jordan, you and all this people, to the land which I am giving to them, to the sons of Israel" (Josh. 1:1-2).

These Scripture passages describe a time when the children of Israel experienced a lot of failure during their 40 years of wandering in the Sinai wilderness. When Moses died, God said, "Quit your crying. Do not remember the things of the past because I'm about to do a new thing in your lives."

You may have endured a lot of failure in your past, but God wants to help you put it behind you so you can move into your future. Sometimes you have to say goodbye to your past so God can do a new thing in your life!

This book is specifically designed as a 30-day "life makeover" plan to help you overcome your past and step into your God-ordained destiny. It is solid and carefully targeted Bible-based discipleship framed in a 30-day format to help you get your past behind you once and for all. It will help you make strategic and *biblical* course corrections for the mistakes you have made, and it will help you overcome all of the failures of the past.

God bless you,
Bishop Dennis Leonard

Day 1

TEN REASONS PEOPLE FAIL

Everyone fails. When failure hits, failure hurts—whether you are tall, short, "weight-challenged," or gracing the cover of some fantasy figure fashion magazine.

We *all* go through failures. When failure comes *your* way, will you overcome it? Will you learn enough from your failure to become what God called you to be?

I have good news for you if failure is dominating your finances, career, relationships or marriage. You don't have to remain a victim. You can *change* direction and do some things that will turn around your life!

After years of work and leadership in the business world and in the ministry, I've discovered there are ten reasons why people fail. Other people may feel there are far more than ten reasons, but most will fall into one of the ten basic errors leading to failure.

The first reason that people fail is because they hold on to the past. God said through the prophet Isaiah, "Behold, I will do something new, now it will spring forth; will you not be aware of it?" (Is. 43:19a, NASB).

Paul the apostle showed us how to handle the past when he said:

> ...but one thing I do: *forgetting what lies behind* and *reaching forward to what lies ahead*, I press on toward the goal for the prize of the upward call of God in Christ Jesus (Phil. 3:13b-14).

God wants to do a new thing in your life. You cannot afford to get stuck in the rut of the past. You will literally be left behind. Put the past behind you—including all of your failures and shortcomings. It is time to move forward.

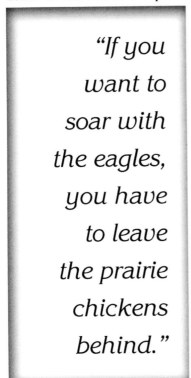

"If you want to soar with the eagles, you have to leave the prairie chickens behind."

A Sad Monument to the Dead Past

You must let go of your failures before God can give you a new beginning. When God sent an angel to give Lot and his family a new beginning, Lot's wife looked back even as she was trying to walk forward (see Gen. 19:26). It cost her everything because she was turned into a pillar of salt—a sad monument to living in the dead past. God had prepared a great future for her, but she was stuck in the past.

If you want to overcome failure in your life, you may have to leave some people behind you as well as some memories. If you want to soar with the eagles, you have to leave the prairie chickens behind.

Learn from your past, but release it and let God take you to a new place. Forget what lies behind and reach forward to what lies ahead.

The second reason that people fail is because of fear. God's Word says you should "walk by faith and not by sight" (2 Cor. 5:7). When fear comes, press on through it by trusting in God.

If you fear financial failure, the enemy of your soul will try to convince you that giving to God is the worst thing you could do. "I am afraid that if I give God a tithe or even an offering right now, then I won't have any money left."

The enemy is a liar and the father of lies. Dismiss his constant claims of doom and gloom and shake off that fear. If you lose the battle to fear, you will never accomplish what God has called you to do.

What does the Bible say about fear? "*For God hath not given us the spirit of fear;* but of *power,* and of *love,* and of *a sound mind*" (2 Tim. 1:7, KJV).

God will help you overcome, no matter what manner of fear comes against you—including the fear of failure, of success, of public speaking, of large crowds, and of loneliness.

Job said, "*For the thing which I greatly feared* is come upon me, and *that which I was afraid of* is come unto me" (Job 3:25, KJV). He believed in his heart that he was going to lose everything he had—*and he did.*

If You Fear It, You Might Get It

I have known people that feared cancer so much that they got it. The thing *you* fear the most may come upon you, too. You *must* overcome those fears by trusting God.

The Apostle Paul said, "Be anxious for nothing, but in everything by prayer and supplication with thanksgiving let your requests be made known to God" (Phil. 4:6, NASB). This my point: You need to worry over nothing and pray over everything.

Fear opens the door of your life for the enemy. As long as you let fear control you, you will never succeed the way God wants you to succeed. Fearful people always fail. That's because fear immobilizes you and it keeps you from stepping out in faith.

Worry is nothing more than a form of fear, so don't worry about anything. Just "cast your cares on the Lord" and trust Him (see 1 Pet. 4:7).

The third reason that people fail is because of negative attitudes. Successful people think differently than unsuccessful people. Negativity is a key difference—unsuccessful people are negative, successful people *are not.* If you are a negative thinker, then you *must* begin to reprogram yourself with the Word of God.

Joshua had a big job to do—he had to fill the shoes of Moses and lead Israel into the Promised Land. How did he do it? What was his secret? He said, "I am going to meditate on God's Word day and night and do all that it says, and God will command success on me" (see Josh. 1:8).

If you are a negative thinker, you must reprogram your mind with God's Word. Get the Word inside of you and meditate on it. Read books that will help your attitude (I've never seen somebody be a success who was not a reader).

Most of us grow up with a negative thought life because most of us were raised by negative people. Poor thinking produces poor results. Good thinking produces good results. The Bible says, "For as [a man] thinketh in his heart, so is he" (Pr. 23:7a).

We don't fail in this life because someone doesn't like us, because of our skin color, or because of our culture. We fail because of our attitudes.

There Is An Attitude Behind Your Words

The children of Israel literally missed out on God's blessings and died in the wilderness because they constantly complained and practiced "grasshopper thinking." Death and life are in the power of the tongue (Pr. 18:21a). There is an attitude behind your words. Turn around your words so your attitude will turn around. It is not what happens *to* you that determines your success; it is what happens *inside* you.

The fourth reason people fail is poor people skills. Whether you are a pastor or a store clerk, poor people skills will cause you to fail. Life is too short not to get along with folk. The church could learn from Wal-Mart—every employee is taught that if they are within ten feet of someone, they must look the person in the eye, smile, and be friendly.

God is not mocked and whatever you sow you will reap (see Gal. 6:7). If you treat people badly, *you* will be treated badly. If you are hard to get along with, I promise you that failure is knocking at your door.

The fifth reason people fail is a lack of focus. In our busy culture, we get so busy that we don't stay focused. Distracted people rarely finish anything. When you stay focused, it's much easier to hit the target.

Set specific, measurable goals in life, and stay focused until you reach them. It is not good enough to shoot at a target; you have to hit it. Increase your focus factor by keeping track of things—use note pads, take notes, capture your thoughts on a digital voice recorder. Keep everything in focus and heading in the right direction.

Focus Makes the Difference

A laser beam is a weak source of energy. It only takes a few watts of power to produce a laser beam, but when that weak beam of light energy is focused into a single stream of light that laser beam can cut through a piece of metal because focus makes the difference. Focus makes the difference.

The sixth reason people fail is because of sin and compromise. There is something about sin and compromise that stops the power of God in a believer's life.

"It is not good enough to shoot at a target; you have to hit it."

The Apostle Peter said, "...like the Holy One who called you, be holy yourselves also in all your behavior" (1 Pet. 1:15 NASB).

The Apostle John said, "Little children, let no one deceive you; the one who practices righteousness is righteous, just as He is righteous; the one who practices sin is of the devil..." (1 John 3:7-8a, NASB).

If you want to overcome failure in your life then tell your boyfriend, "No wed, no bed." Put God first in everything. If you are trapped in an addiction, take the mask off and admit your problem. Confess your sin and get help from your family in Christ.

Sin stops success and blocks prosperity. It may take a day, a year, or a decade, but it *will* happen. Put God first in your life. If you are committing adultery, embezzling money, or cheating on your taxes—repent *now* and start fresh.

James the apostle said, "Therefore, to one who knows the right thing to do, and does not do it, to him it is sin" (Jas. 4:17, NASB).

This is also God's definition of *compromise*. Do the right thing and prosper. Compromise and suffer the consequences.

The seventh reason people fail is because they make excuses for their failure. Excuses are a "family trait." At the beginning of the human family tree, Adam pointed at Eve and told God, "That woman *You* gave me made me eat the forbidden fruit." The fallen nature of man automatically blames somebody else. Eve said, "Well, it wasn't my fault. The serpent tempted me. He made me do it. He tricked me" (see Gen. 3:12-13).

It wasn't my Fault...I've Been Framed

When we fail, we tend to point fingers at others and assign blame. "If only my boss would have done something...if my ex would have done something else...it was my parents' fault...." The classic jailhouse phrase is a "family" favorite for humanity—"It wasn't my fault, I've been framed!"

Stop making excuses for your failure and stop pointing your finger. According to Isaiah the prophet, the Lord will answer your prayers "...if you remove the yoke from your midst, *the pointing of the finger* [in blame] ..." (Is. 58:9, NASB).

Quit blaming the white man, the black man, and the tax man. Quit blaming your parents, your in-laws, and your outlaws. Admit your sins and failures so God will be released to help you.

When you blame others, it becomes an excuse not to change. Take responsibility for your actions as your first step to overcoming failure.

The eighth reason people fail is they resist change. You must *change* if you want to overcome failure and make progress in your life. Change is rarely comfortable. It will stretch you because it represents a sacrifice for you. If a particular change isn't awkward to you, it probably isn't enough of a change.

Naaman was a Syrian army captain who suffered from leprosy. He came to a prophet of God for a cure, but he had a preset idea of how prophets are supposed to work. When Elisha the prophet told him to dip seven times in the muddy Jordan River, he refused. He had to swallow his pride and change his thinking to receive a miracle (see 2 Kings 5:9-14).

Go Back and Take the Test Again...

If you experience failure but don't change; then you have not learned your lesson. Get ready—you are about to go back and take the test again! Once the lesson is learned, you will quit blaming other people, take off your mask, and honestly examine yourself.

Most people resist change because they're afraid of the unknown. But only a crazy person would do the same year after year and expect different results in their life. Only a crazy person would go a certain direction and think it's going to be different this time.

The ninth reason people fail is they do not plan to succeed. If you plan for nothing, then you get precisely that—nothing. Jesus warned us to *count the cost first* if we want to build something.

> For which one of you, when he wants to build a tower, does not first sit down and calculate the cost, to see if he has enough to complete it? Otherwise, when he has laid a foundation, and is not able to finish, all who observe it begin to ridicule him, "This man began to build and was not able to finish." Or what king, when he sets out to meet another king in battle, will not first sit down and take counsel whether he is strong enough with ten thousand men to encounter the one coming against him with twenty thousand? (Luke 14:28-31, NASB).

How can you build a house, build a marriage, or build the Kingdom of God in your children if you don't count the cost? No matter what you do or dream, *you must count the cost.*

Did You Plan to Succeed or Plan to Fail?

Have you counted the cost in your life? In a sense, everyone plans. You either plan to succeed, or you plan to fail (through your *lack* of planning). Since nothing of worth comes free in this life, you have to make a plan before you do anything. There is always a price to pay if you want to be successful in marriage, ministry, or business.

The Lord basically told Habakkuk the prophet, "Write down the vision and make it plain!" (Hab. 2:2). If you want to succeed financially, then you must plan for it—and write down that plan. Figure out how much money is coming in and how much must go out each month.

Write out a spending plan—a budget—and then live by it as well as you can. You will probably discover that success doesn't always depend on how *much* money you make as on how you use what you have, and on your ability to count the cost before leaping into debt blindly or making unplanned purchases.

> *"Since nothing of worth comes free in this life, you have to make a plan before you do anything."*

"Well Pastor, God wants me to own a house, so I believe He will get me one." Don't stop there. Honestly examine your finances and figure out your budget. Do your homework, establish a plan, and then work the plan.

If you decide to get married, seek out qualified, Bible-based pre-marital counseling. Count the cost carefully, because you and your future partner are carrying all kinds of baggage into your marriage (this is normal, but *remaining* that way is not). Counseling will help you make a plan to work through all your personal issues and hang-ups so you can become what God wants you to be in your marriage.

When you begin to plan for something, avoid *unrealistic* expectations. Set goals that you can attain. If you want to lose 75 pounds, then start with a realistic goal of losing five pounds per month.

The tenth reason people fail is they give up too soon. Everyone has felt like quitting from time to time. As a Christian, you must believe that God is working out everything in your life. Remember that it is darkest just before the dawn. The Lord always has a way of showing up "just in time."

The best things are often born or created in the worst times. The apostle Paul wrote most of the Epistles while he was in prison.

Ten Reasons People Fail

Florence Nightingale reorganized the hospitals of England from her own sick bed, and Booker T. Washington was greatly disadvantaged and yet he built a great school. George Washington Carver suffered great discrimination, but he became a great scientist. Martin Luther King Jr. was told to keep his mouth shut and be quiet, but he kept declaring the truth and led a revolution in the 1960's.

Tough Times Breed Tough Leaders

Louis Pasteur was partially paralyzed when he found the cure for many diseases. Abraham Lincoln was raised in poverty but he led our nation through the dark years of the Civil War. Franklin D. Roosevelt was stricken with infantile paralysis but he led America during World War II. Don't give up just because things are tough. Tough times breed tough leaders.

Glen Cunningham was burned so badly that his doctor's said he would never walk again. Yet in 1934, he became the first human being to run the mile in less than four minutes, setting a world record!

Beethoven the composer was deaf. Thomas Edison, the inventor of the telephone, was deaf. Charles Dickens the author was lame and couldn't walk. Plato the philosopher was a hunchback, and Sir Walter Scott the author couldn't walk.

When you serve the Lord Jesus Christ, *failure is not the end*. It is nothing more than the mark of a new beginning!

Failure is a signal that changes are needed. Decide right now that when failure comes, you will make the necessary changes and trust God in a new way.

(We are dedicated to serving you and God's kingdom in any way we can. Don't hesitate to contact us through our Internet website at www.DLministries.com).

∞ Failure Is not the End ∞

Day 2

PRINCIPLES TO
OVERCOME FAILURE

My flesh and my heart may fail. But God is the strength of my heart and my portion forever (Ps. 73:26).

You cannot experience a measure of success in your life without also experiencing failure. The only way to avoid failure is to die, and the only way to experience success is to *learn from your failures*.

When you put God first in your life, every failure becomes a step-ping-stone to God's destiny for you. We know that God's Word says, "The steps of a good man are ordered by the Lord..." (Ps. 37:23, KJV). He also said, "'For I know the plans that I have for you,' declares the Lord, 'plans for welfare and not for calamity to give you a future and a hope'" (Jer. 29:11).

If you love the Lord and have surrendered your life totally to him, you have an "edge" in life. God Himself is directing your steps toward "a future and a hope." Even if that path takes you though failure, every challenge or fall becomes a stepping-stone when you are in God's hands.

Each time failure comes along (and it will), *you* must decide whether you will learn from your mistakes or not. I've discovered some key principles in God's Word that will help you overcome failure and become truly successful in life.

Eight Principles For Overcoming Failure

Principle #1: Do not let fear control you. You love God, Who created the universe; and He holds your life in His hands. The Bible says, "For God hath not given us the spirit of fear; but of power, and of love, and of a sound mind" (2 Tim. 1:7, KJV). Do not let fear control you.

Rest assured your mortal enemy will try to get you to operate in fear, because he knows that when you operate in fear you are bound to fail. Faith and fear are absolute opposites.

The enemy will work overtime to plant *fear* in your mind about your relationships, your job, your health, your finances, and even the certainty of death. As a Christian, you know that even death has lost its hold over you!

God told the children of Israel as they were going into their promised land, "Don't look at the giants around you. Don't turn to the right and don't turn to the left. Be strong and courageous." You must make the same choices!

Worry is just another form of fear. Why worry about things over which you have no control? Do what the Bible says. Live life freely… "casting all your anxiety upon Him, because He cares for you" (1 Pet. 5:7). If you can do something about a problem, then *do it.* Accept the things you cannot change and *trust God.*

Principle #2: Check your attitudes. Anytime you experience failure, make sure you check your attitude thermometer. If all is well, you will still be convinced that failure is only temporary. The right attitude

12

says, "This, too, shall pass." The enemy may seem to be winning today, but the God in you says, "This too shall pass."

It is amazing to see how one person can look at a situation and see an opportunity while the next person looks at the *same situation* but sees only an impossibility. It is all about attitude. Remember: Attitude determines how far and how high you go in this life.

Principle #3: Do not make excuses. Some people blame everyone else for their failures. Until you accept responsibility for your actions, you will always live in failure. Do not play the blame game.

Some people go from failure to failure because they are full of excuses. No more excuses. Close the door on that blame-shifting mentality. Honesty is the best policy: Take responsibility for your failures *and* for your own success.

In the very beginning, Adam tried to blame his failure on Eve and on God (for giving him Eve in the first place). Eve joined the blame game by blaming her wrong choices and failure on the serpent. Whatever you do, don't play the blame game.

> *"Attitude determines how far and how high you go in this life."*

Principle #4: Never let failure get inside you. We mentioned this example earlier, but it deserves a second mention: "Why do ships sink? The stuff on the outside gets on the inside."

Why do people sink? They let the stuff on the outside get on the inside. They get bogged down in their failures, negative attitudes, and the past. And they fail. Never let failure get inside you because then you will start feeling sorry for yourself.

Even if you have experienced a whole string of failures, do not let it get inside you. Remember that failure becomes a mere stepping-stone on God's path for your destiny.

"I've made up my mind; I'm going to trust in the Lord. I have failed, but that was then and this is now. This is a stepping-stone to where God is taking me, and He always lifts me higher than where I was before."

One thing is for sure: every successful person has had failures (and negative critics who thought their future held nothing but more failure). They refused to see themselves as failures and persevered.

Albert Einstein was told by one of his teachers that he would never amount to anything. He was actually expelled from school because he was "so slow." Can you imagine what would have happened if that young student had let that teacher's foolish opinion get inside him? Today, we recognize Albert Einstein as one the world's greatest geniuses!

The artist, Vincent Van Gough, sold only one painting in his entire lifetime. Today his paintings sell for millions of dollars. He was a success and didn't know it.

Eddie Arcaro is arguably the world's most famous jockey, amassing one of the most successful horse racing careers in history. Yet, he lost 250 races before he ever won one!

In 1954, Hank Aaron played his first professional baseball game. In his first game, he never even hit the ball his first five times at bat. Fortunately, he didn't quit. He went on to become the all-time home-run king of professional baseball (as of this writing).

Principle #5: Change yourself. Wise people don't limit their focus to their strong points in life. They constantly examine their lives for *weak* points as well. It is the weak areas of your life that will keep you from becoming a success. Seek out your weakness so you can do something about it. *Change yourself* before someone else has to do it.

Everyone has at least one weakness (and most of us have a long list of them). The way you deal with your weaknesses may determine the way you deal with other parts of your life.

Principles to Overcome Failure

If your life is not going the way you want it to go, then change something. Search out your weaknesses, seek God for direction, and change yourself.

The only way to fully achieve your potential is to honestly face yourself and recognize your flaws. You can reach your potential tomorrow if you'll dedicate yourself to change today. Change yourself and prosper.

Principle #6: Learn from your mistakes. If you will see "failure" as your teacher, then you can learn from your mistakes and make necessary changes.

The average person who starts a business fails three or four times before they make it a success. That is why you can't let failure stop you. Every failure means you are that much closer to success.

Why should we learn from mistakes? The truth is that most of us learn very little from our successes! We learn the *most* from our failures. It has been my failures that have made me what I am, not my successes. If anything, my success fed my arrogance. My failures taught me to humble myself and showed me exactly where I needed to change.

The road to success has been paved with bricks of failure, and every brick of failure has taken me higher and further into my destiny with God. I do not like to fail, but my failures helped make me what I am. I wish I didn't fail, but I did and I've learned from what I failed.

Every failure was difficult and some were heartbreaking. Failure isn't fun, but it is necessary. So *learn* from each failure so you won't have to go there again!

Principle #7: Let go of the past. People who hold to the past never go forward to the future. You know who they are because they constantly talk about the past and they seem to live while looking backwards. I'm through looking back.

I have never met anyone who was successful that lived in the past. The past is the past, whether it is dominated by failures or successes. Isaiah the prophet said under the inspiration of God, "Do not call to mind the former things, or ponder things of the past. Behold, I will do something new..." (Is. 43:18-19a).

Quit thinking about it. Quit meditating on it. Quit talking about it. Trust God for a new thing in your life!

Principle #8: Never give up. Paul said, "I have fought the good fight, I have finished the course, I have kept the faith" (2 Tim. 4:7). I say it another way, "Paul was too legit to quit."

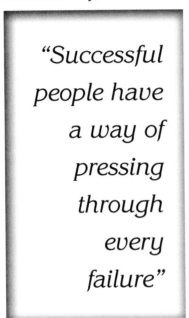

"Successful people have a way of pressing through every failure"

After a major snowstorm dumped six feet of snow in front of our garage doors, I waded out there with a snow shovel to rescue our cars—one shovel full at a time. More than 90 minutes later, it didn't look like I had even made a dent in the project. Then I heard the Lord say, "Son, that's the mountain of your past failures in front of you. You can get rid of those failures one by one, if you don't quit."

I was ready to quit about halfway through, but something inside of me said, *If I quit now, my failures will haunt me all of my life.* Then God said, "Son, keep on." Later, as I leaned on the shovel to catch my breath, the Lord said, "Son, it is not the fastest one that wins the race." He wanted me to remain steadfast while He continued His work in me, removing the weight of past failures. It is not how fast you go. Just keep on trusting God and *never quit.*

Successful people have a way of pressing through every failure—they refuse to quit despite their mistakes. And they never see *themselves* as a mistake or a failure.

(If you are wrestling with the weight of past failure and would like some support, don't hesitate to contact us through our Internet website at www.DLministries.com).

16

Day 3

FEAR AND FAILURE

Whoever believes that Jesus is the Christ is born of God; and whoever loves the Father loves the child born of Him. By this we know that we love the children of God, when we love God and observe His commandments. For this is the love of God, that we keep His commandments; and His commandments are not burdensome. For whatever is born of God overcomes the world; and this is the victory that has overcome the world—our faith. And who is the one who overcomes the world, but he who believes that Jesus is the Son of God? (1 John 5: 1-5).

We do four things when we become born again that prove we are born of God: We love God, we love the children of God, we keep the commandments of God, and we overcome the world through our faith in God.

You know you are born again when you want to do God's will, even when your flesh fights you every step of the way. If the "want to" isn't there, then I seriously question whether or not you were "reborn to."

Something is wrong if you live like you used to live and don't feel any kind of guilt or conviction of sin. This is also true if you don't love your brethren.

Being born again does not mean you will never fail; it means that your heart has been changed, and you want to do right at all times.

Once you give your life to God, His commandments are no longer "burdensome" or so heavy that they weigh you down. Now that you love the Lord, He has written His commandments on your heart.

It is no longer a burden to obey God when your heart burns to please and bless Him, and to never grieve His Spirit through sin. Love produces more love. God's loving presence in your heart makes it possible to keep those commandments through grace and love for Him.

Your faith in Him is more than enough for any situation because the Bible says your *faith* in the Lord will cause you to *overcome* the spirit of the world. This is where things seem to fall apart in the modern church.

Since he knows we cannot please God without faith, our spiritual enemy is always trying to trick us into walking in fear. He does everything he can to steal our faith through deception or at least confuse us with misinformation.

We Lay Down the Cross to Pickup Our List of Offenses

He wants us to believe that God is mad at us, or that He shows favorites by ignoring us while helping Sister So-and-So. He wants us to get so offended at our brother or sister that we lay down the cross to pickup our list of offenses. He wants us to focus on what *might happen* if things go wrong instead of what *did* happen at Calvary.

I spent most of my life fearing that something bad was going to happen to me. My past experiences and sins helped produce the fear, but that fear dominated my life.

Fear and Failure

Even now I occasionally wake up with the feeling that something bad is going to happen, but I've learned how to pray and cast my cares on the Lord.

The only way to be what God wants you to be is to make the decision to *walk by faith and not by sight.*

The enemy knows when you have *real faith.* He also knows that when you put *faith and action together,* then nothing is impossible for you!

The enemy knows that my strength comes from the Word. That's why He wants me to read the newspaper every morning instead of the Word. The enemy knows that if I can get caught up in reading some novel rather than reading the Word, he knows he can keep the Word out of my heart.

"Faith is a decision, not a feeling."

You will never have any spiritual strength to your life until you get in the Word (and the Word gets into you). You can show up at the church seven days a week, but unless the Word is inside you, you will not have the strength to overcome.

You Are Destined To Succeed When You Put God First

Many Christians seem to live under a spirit of failure, and usually I find that they don't put God first in some area of their lives. You are destined to succeed when you put God first.

If you tend to be a negative person, understand it is the spirit of fear trying to get a grip on your life. Faith is a decision, not a feeling. If God said to do it, then do it whether you like it or not. You have to decide to walk in faith because it won't happen by accident.

Decide right now: "I will be a person of faith, not a person of fear. If God said it, then I stand on it."

Put God first, even in the least significant areas of your life. King Saul learned the hard way that *to obey is better than sacrifice* (see

1 Sam. 15:22b). It is better to obey the first time than to disobey and then come back to God saying, "I'm sorry, Lord."

Willful disobedience always produces failure at some level. It may happen in your relationships, your finances, on your job, or in your church—*but it will happen.*

God promised Abraham and his descendents that as long as they were careful to do all He commanded, then they would be blessed, highly favored and empowered to prosper.

You Become a Slave To Whatever You Worship and Obey

Over time, the children of Israel *disobeyed* and deserted God to worship idols, exchanging their faith for fear. As a result, they lived in destruction for 400 years as slaves of Pharaoh. *You become a slave to whatever you worship and obey.*

God sent Moses to deliver the children of Israel from Pharaoh, but they took their fearful slave mentality with them. After crossing the wilderness of sin (a well-named geographic location), the children of Israel could actually see their promised land.

Only a hundred yards away from the land of promise and their divine destiny, those people let their fear and negativity *overcame* their faith! It was supposed to be the other way around. They refused to cross the Jordan by faith because they didn't believe God would fight for them.

Their reverse faith (fear) brought a curse upon their heads to wander in the wilderness until that entire adult generation died. *Fearful people always fail. Negative people always fall.*

If you plan to make some changes in obedience to God, get ready for a battle. No one changes for good without a battle with evil. Your flesh wants everything to stay the same with sacrifice-free, self-centered living.

Your flesh will resist change to the bitter end. That is why the Bible says we must "lay aside" the old man of the flesh. The old man is already dead—it was crucified with Christ on the cross (see Rom. 6:6).

God has His way of getting our attention. If you stop short of faith and turn back in fear, God just might let you wander back into the wilderness *because that's the place He talks to you*. He keeps working in the midst of your failure and fear to increase your faith. The wilderness of failure and crisis is the place He begins to change you.

Once you start making some changes, keep operating in faith and work out the fear. Continue to believe God's promise that in due season you will reap your harvest.

God Takes Your Complaining Personally

Negative people become their own worst enemy because they absolutely torment themselves (and everyone around them). The problem with being a negative complainer is that **God takes it personally.** He sees through all of the words to the heart and He knows that you don't have faith in Him.

"If you've grown tired of your own complaining, then it is time to get over your past."

If you've grown tired of your own complaining, then it is time to get over your past. If you want to step into the present and march out of the wilderness toward your inheritance, then it is time to make some changes by faith.

The children of Israel became discouraged in the wilderness the second time around. Wandering wears you out. It is in the depths of struggle that you make the most of your hard decisions: What am I going to do? Am I going to complain and wander around in negativity the rest of my life, or am I going to change? *Will I walk in faith or in fear?*

The Bible says, "Fear not" 366 times: "Fear not, for I have redeemed you." "Fear not, for I've called you by name." "Fear not, even though the earth should quake and fall into the sea." "Fear not, what man can do to you?"

With 366 declarations, there is an "I fear not" for every day of the week including leap year! Are you getting the message? *Fear not!*

Your flesh loves the easy life, and it will beg you to quit when the going gets tough. Don't quit, begin to exercise your faith in the *middle* of your trial so you can fulfill your calling as a *world overcomer!*

If anxiety seizes your life, then perhaps you dropped the shield of faith and yielded to a spirit of fear. Panic attacks will paralyze your life if you allow your will to switch back from faith to fear. When panic hits you, you think, "My God, all is lost right here."

Face Your Enemy Head-On

In those crisis moments, take a deep breath and make the choice to trust in the Lord with *all* of your heart. Then face your enemy head-on and run to the battle fully equipped.

Don't run to a battle of faith armed with a bottle of aspirin—arm yourself with winning strategies, insightful intelligence information on the enemy's tactics, offensive weapons, and defensive body armor. It is all there in Ephesians 6.

You need the full armor of God—gird your loins with truth, put on the breastplate of righteousness, put your shoes on (the ones labeled "the preparation of the gospel of peace"), pick up the shield of faith, the helmet of salvation, and the sword of the Spirit (God's Word).

It amazes me to see Christians who "hear and receive the Word with gladness" turn around and refuse to obey the Word in the next breath. It shocks me that born-again Christians could receive all of the promises that God offers to them and yet demand the freedom to do whatever they want to do.

The devil's plan is for you to live in sin and fear so you will live in perpetual failure. He wants to recruit you as his own professional complainer planted in God's camp. When you begin to suffer from living in constant failure, he deceives you into blaming God and complaining instead of having faith in His power to heal, deliver, and transform your life.

Fear and Failure

According to Rom. 14:23, "Anything that is not of faith is sin." That goes for every religious act we perform in church or in the soup kitchen. If it is not of *faith,* then it is sin.

The More Trouble Comes, The More I Will Trust Him

I am determined to hang onto my faith. I'm determined to be careful in what I say because I have made a lifelong decision to change. Disappointment may come, but still I will trust in Him. The ride in God's boat may be rougher than I want it to be, but still I will trust in Him. The more trouble comes, the more I will trust Him.

You cannot afford to let anxiety get a death-grip on your life. The Bible says, "For God hath not given us the spirit of fear; but of power, and of love, and of a sound mind" (2 Tim. 1:7, KJV).

I am casting *all* of my cares, concerns, and fears on the Lord (see 1 Pet. 5:7). Throw your fears as far from you as possible. "Worry, get off of me. Get away from me."

You may be in a difficult place at this moment, but *this too shall pass.* Trouble won't last forever because God is going to bring you out. Block that spirit of failure with the shield of faith. Failure is not the end if you remove fear and realize that failure can be God's stepping stone for promotion.

Fear is a doorway for the enemy to come into your life, but faith is the gateway of God for heaven to come to earth through you. What door will you step through?

(Don't let fear dictate your future. We are dedicated to serving you and God's kingdom in any way we can. If you feel we can help, don't hesitate to contact us through our Internet website at www.DLministries.com).

∽ FAILURE IS NOT THE END ∽

Day 4

FAILURE LEADS TO POTENTIAL

> But [Jesus] looked at them and said, "What then is this
> that is written, 'THE STONE WHICH THE BUILDERS
> REJECTED, THIS BECAME THE CHIEF CORNER
> stone'? Everyone who falls on that stone will be broken
> to pieces; but on whomever it falls, it will scatter him
> like dust" (Lk. 20:17-18).

Failure may be one of the most important ingredients in your life! Without it, most of us wouldn't give God a second thought. We dread failure; we lose sleep at night wrestling with endless anxiety over the possibility that we might fail.

The problem is that the human race left the Garden of Eden with a virtually unlimited supply of arrogance and pride hidden in our bloodline. Our wild crop of self-importance flourishes as long as things go well. It often takes a healthy dose of *failure* to finally open our hearts to God's love and forgiveness.

We don't like the verse that says, "for all have sinned and fall short of the glory of God" (Rom. 3:23). We almost believe we *are* god-like, or at the very least, that we can get along just fine without God's help. It seems failure is the most effective way to rein in pride and humble arrogance.

The "Leonard paraphrase" of the opening Scripture reference from Luke reads: "If you decide to fall on the Lord Jesus Christ and come to Him in your failures, He will put your life back together. If you chose to do your own thing and to be your own god, eventually either you will destroy yourself or life will destroy you."

There is something inside each of us that wants to be *in charge*. We don't like to hear anyone tell us what to do. Unfortunately, God cannot do much for us until He sees a real brokenness in our hearts.

Failure is God's warning beacon signaling your need for change in your life. It warns you, "Begin to evaluate your life. Change your direction." If it were not for failure, very few of us would even begin to be what God has called us to be. It takes something *painful* to overcome the drugging effects of self-centered pride and arrogance.

Logically, what would a bright person do if things weren't going well on the job? He would investigate, isolate the problem, and *fix it* just as a mechanic would fix an engine. He would go to the boss and say, "I realize I am not making you happy. What can I do to make you happy? What can I do to get this thing turned around? Tell me how I can change the way I do things to make this organization more efficient, profitable, and healthy."

The Admission of Failure Is Beneath Us

We immediately reject such an idea because we are not engines—we are living beings with emotions and pride to protect. The admission of failure is beneath us. We would rather cling to our pride and arrogance than hold a job. God allows us to experience the pain of failure just to bring us down from the clouds of self and to capture our attention.

Failure Leads to Potential

So failure is a vital part of healthy life. Every man or woman in the Bible experienced failure. Failure doesn't mean that God can't use you; it almost seems to be a *prerequisite*, a requirement that must be met if God is ever to use you.

Failure says, "Wait a minute. Back up and regroup, and look at yourself. This is *not* working, so face the facts. You need to make some changes, go on, and trust God."

One of failure's greatest functions is to lead us to our potential. Unfortunately, our own ideas often become the greatest obstacles blocking our road to destiny.

If you sincerely desire to be used by God, then expect failure to come into your life, because it's going to show you where you need to make some changes. It propels you to the point where you humble yourself and cry out to the Lord.

> *"Failure helps us realize that we can't make it without the Lord."*

Failure helps us realize that we can't make it without the Lord. When we forget the previous humility lesson or focus too much on self, God has a way of applying gentle pressure on us to make changes in our lives.

Will You Give Up Your Agenda For God's Agenda?

When you are broken by failure, it is amazing to see how easy it is to give up your agenda for God's agenda. Brokenness and failure work together to help us serve rather than expect to be served.

The only people God can use effectively are people with *servant's hearts*. People come to us all the time wanting to be in the ministry and join our staff. They generally have some talent or abilities that they are sure they can use for God. They don't realize that I am looking for a servant's heart more than a powerful minister's bag of tricks. Unfortunately, very few of these people actually have servant's hearts.

A servant's heart doesn't need a position or constant applause from the people served. A servant's heart says, "Lord, show me a place to serve. If I never get patted on the back, if nobody ever says, 'You did a great job,' it is okay with me. I am here to serve You before anything else."

In the early days, I had my life all planned out. "God, You know I'd do anything for you. Just don't ever ask me to be a Pastor. I'll even preach, but don't ask me to pastor people, because they're a lot of problems."

God said, "You have got your plans and I have Mine." When I began to find out what God's plans were I had to say, "Okay God, change my heart." Once God's hand is on you, you will never be happy until you fully submit to God's perfect will for your life.

Blessed, Broken and Multiplied

A powerful three-step process was revealed in the last supper: Jesus blessed the bread, He broke the bread, and then He multiplied the bread. Jesus submitted Himself to the same process, and so must you. God *blessed* you when you gave your life to Him. He *breaks* you in your failures and voluntary surrender.

His goal is to *multiply* you through the good fruit of your life, your joyful witness to the unsaved, and your consistent stand for godliness in a dark generation. (When you submit to this process, He is actually multiplying or duplicating Himself through your life!)

The sinful woman with the alabaster box who came to anoint Jesus had to break the jar before she could pour it all out. She was just as broken as the box of anointment, and it was her brokenness that blessed Jesus the most. Unless you are broken, you can't be poured out. Unless you are broken, you cannot be used the way God wants to use you.

You may be walking on a road paved with the bricks of your failures right now, but be encouraged. Failure is *not* the end. Your failures

Failure Leads to Potential

are literally leading you to your potential! The turnaround begins as you learn from your mistakes so you won't go there again.

Make no mistake: God uses your failure to capture your attention. That may be the only time you will listen to His quiet voice. It is in middle of your failures that you begin to change and grow.

Failure isn't God's first choice for communication. He begins by guiding and correcting us through His Word, through our brothers and sisters in Christ, and through His leaders. If we don't listen at this level, in comes failure (and the pain associated with it).

Some Promotions Must Come Through Perseverance In a Storm

Even people with good "spiritual listening skills" will face failure and crisis from time to time. Some promotions and preparations for leadership must come through perseverance in a storm or crisis. We all have to endure storms in our lives so we know what kind of faith we have.

Failure can lead you to your potential *if* you will learn from your mistakes. God loves us too much to leave us in our fleshly condition. He is determined to conform us to the image of His Son, and that means that some unpleasant things have to go.

Out go the unpleasant attitudes, selfishness, inflated pride, uncontrolled anger and rage, fear, and gossip. He points out the friends and associates harboring deadly attitudes and habits and tells us to sever the relationships before they infect us with their afflictions. In the process, God allows failure to come into our lives.

We need God's help in every area. How do I raise the kids and help guide my grandkids? How should I invest my money, and who can I trust to help me? How can I restore financial integrity?

All we need to do is *confess our failures* to the Lord and He will strengthen us every single day.

Preachers are especially bad about promoting the idea they don't have any weaknesses. Behind closed doors, we preachers struggle with things that would amaze you. This much is sure: Every one of us walks with a limp.

I don't care if we are preachers, policemen, doctors, or judges—we all have a limp. Every one of us needs to go to the Lord and say, "Lord, I need help with this part of my life...."

You Will Have to Make Some Changes

God uses the weak things in this world to confound the wise (see 1 Cor. 1:27). The fact that you are human and have some weaknesses does not disqualify you with God—as long as you realize you will have to make some changes.

> ## "When I am weak, He is Strong."

I am not a leader because I am perfect or especially strong. I lead because I am weak and I know how strong *He* is. I've settled the question—*I know I can't make it without Him*. I constantly ask Him, "Lord, what do You want me to do? Show me Your plan."

I'm not ashamed to admit that I am weak and I need His strength. I openly confess that without God's help, I wouldn't make it.

I failed God before I was saved, and I failed Him after I was saved. However, I have learned to change. I am the righteousness of God *in Christ*, and I know that God isn't mad at me. In fact, I have learned that *when I am weak, He is strong* (see 2 Cor. 5:21, 12:9; Jn. 3:16).

It seems that we all have areas in our lives that cause us to limp. God knows you need to lean on Him. He knows what you need to help you make changes in your life.

Paul the apostle revealed his "limp" in his second letter to the Corinthians:

> ...to keep me from exalting myself, there was given me a thorn in the flesh, a messenger of Satan to buffet me—to keep me from exalting myself! Concerning this I entreated the Lord three times that it might depart from me. And He has said to me, "My grace is

sufficient for you, *for power is perfected in weakness*" (2 Cor. 12:7b-9).

Is Pride Ruling or Influencing My Life?

Paul says his "thorn in the flesh" was the constant persecution he suffered for the sake of the gospel, the external forces coming against him. Anytime you go through failure in your life, stop and ask, "Is pride ruling or influencing any area of my life, Lord? Do I need to make a correction?"

I wish I could tell you that I don't have any weaknesses, but it is my weaknesses that make me realize, "Lord, I can't make it without You." God has called me to lead people who have problems, to show them they are no longer victims but more than conquerors through Christ.

If you feel broken and discarded because of failure in your life, be encouraged that God is getting ready to put you back together again. You must go through some struggles to qualify as a candidate to be used by God! How else would you touch others who are enduring real pain in their lives?

God chooses people with great disadvantages and weaknesses and transforms them to perform great tasks requiring great faith. Paul said, "God has chosen the foolish things of the world to shame the wise, and God has chosen the weak things of the world to shame the things which are strong" (1 Cor. 1:27).

God can't show up until you confess your sin and you humble yourself before Him. Let Him strengthen you where you are weak. When you surrender your life to the Lord, your disadvantages become advantages and your strengths may become liabilities. Failure leads to potential if you keep a humble attitude before God.

I firmly believe that when God really gets a hold of your heart and you begin to make the right changes, then good things will begin to show up in your life. Failure isn't the end; it is the pathway of God leading to potential.

Trust the big God you serve. He isn't "guessing" or "hoping." He knows what He is doing. He is the Almighty God who knows *exactly* what to do to bring you through your failures and into your full potential!

(God wants you to fulfill your kingdom potential, and so do we. Don't hesitate to contact us through our Internet website at www.DLministries.com).

Day 5

ATTITUDES WILL MAKE YOU OR BREAK YOU

Seasoned coaches in almost every sport preach one truth more than any other—*attitude is everything.* Although I must insist that *Christ* is everything, I agree that attitude is crucial once you put God first. The Bible says, "As [a man] thinks within himself, so he is" (Pr. 23:7a).

What do you think? Do you believe you win in the end, or do you think life is just an endless struggle to avoid inevitable failure and postpone a hopeless death? Your attitude on this question will directly affect your altitude in life.

Count on it: You will face some troubles in your life. Do you have a heart attitude and inner conviction that God will eventually cause you to win? I try to make the changes needed in my life to keep my attitude high where my Lord resides. I proclaim out loud, "My best days are still ahead of me!"

What about you? Do you live by God's promises or by your failures? Do you set your attitudes each day by the look of the circumstances

> *"...if you develop an attitude of gratitude and trust in the Lord, then your whole life will change!"*

coming your way or by God's faithfulness in your life? *Excuse me, but your attitude is showing.*

Put the Lord first in your life and believe God's Word when it declares, "The steps of a man are established by the Lord; and He delights in his way" (Ps. 37:23).

Allow your faith in God's faithfulness to change your attitude about the challenges facing you. Again, the Bible says you and I *are* what we think in our hearts.

You will never go anywhere in your life as long as you think negatively. On the other hand, if you develop an attitude of gratitude and trust in the Lord, then your whole life will change! Take your cue from Paul the apostle, who wrote these words in times of turmoil and distress:

But *thanks be to God*, who *always leads us in His triumph* in Christ, and manifests *through us* the sweet aroma of the knowledge of Him in every place (2 Cor. 2:14).

If your attitude determines your altitude, then "grasshopper attitudes" must produce very low-altitude flights for us. In the previous chapter, we noted that the children of Israel practiced "grasshopper thinking." They entered the Wilderness with Moses after living as slaves to Egypt for many generations.

These descendants of Jacob had been beaten down and told they were no good from birth—until God set them free. Nevertheless, they held onto their negative thinking and just kept complaining even though they personally experienced miracle after miracle.

Attitudes Will Make You Or Break You

They Refused to Shake Their Slave Mentality

When faced with the challenge of hostile people in the Promised Land, the adult generation refused to shake their slave mentality. They ignored God's words, and still thought of themselves as grasshoppers and of their opponents as giants.

That generation's negative, doubt-filled thinking earned its members a one-way lifetime pass to the Wilderness where they died marching in a circle for forty years (see Num. 14:1-34).

You have a dangerous dose of wilderness mentality if you are usually negative or complaining about something. Get the cure immediately!

Dig deep in God's Word and find out what *He* says about you and your purpose on earth. Doubt says, "I can't do anything right. Everything always goes wrong for me." Faith—which is really a *God-centered* attitude—says, "I can do all things through Christ which strengtheneth me" (Phil. 4:13, KJV).

Quit saying, "I can't." God says you *can*. Begin by doing everything that *you can do*—then allow Him to do what you cannot do. The basic process is the same whether you want to lose weight, invest wisely, raise your children biblically, witness boldly, or start a business. Do your research in God's Word and in other sources. Pray. Then act.

This is a new day, so reprogram your mind with God's Word and make some changes in your life.

My Best Days Are Still Ahead!

God loves you even if you are a complainer, but He won't do much for you and success will be rare. As long as you are negative, *you will stay in the wilderness and outside of your promised land*. It is better to have a faith report than an evil negative report. Look at your future, smile in the face of your past, and proclaim, "Because God loves me, my best days are still ahead!"

The real challenge is to keep a good attitude even while you are still in a wilderness situation. If you keep a good attitude, God will bring you out. If you just keep going in circles all of your life, perhaps you should stop and ask yourself, "Do I have a wilderness mentality?"

Make no mistake: *The attitude you have right now is going to take you someplace.* You will either climb higher or fall lower. Choose God's way. You don't have to go from failure to failure. *In Christ, you can break free from that negative cycle.*

Do Your Words Trap and Curse or Deliver and Bless?

The Lord wants you to have so much faith in Him that you speak a good report even when the odds are against you. Since the power of life and death are in the tongue, you can be trapped and cursed by your own words or *delivered and blessed* by them. It is your choice.

The Bible says, "*Humble yourselves*, therefore, under the mighty hand of God, that He may *exalt you* at the proper time, *casting all your anxiety upon Him*, because He cares for you" (1 Pet. 5:6-7). Jesus said, "But seek ye first the kingdom of God, and his righteousness; and all these things [your need for food, shelter, clothing, health, and wealth] shall be added unto you" (Mt. 6:33, KJV).

Stop believing the worst. The trials of today are your training ground for victories tomorrow! Change your attitude—God is taking you somewhere.

You learn how to change in your wilderness, not in your Promised Land. You learn to forgive in times of trouble, not in the good times.

Attitude is the Number 1 reason people succeed in life. There are millionaires situated all across the country who accumulated wealth *without* any higher education. Their *attitude* was their greatest investment asset.

Attitude is *also* the Number 1 reason people *fail* in life. Bad attitudes may get you fired from your job, land you in divorce court, or plant you in a prison cell.

Life is too short to be living with a bad attitude. Your attitude may literally affect everyone around you. Negative attitudes produce negative results, but positive attitudes produce positive results. Either way, your attitude can become contagious. What attitude do you want to spread around in Christ's name? "As a man thinketh in his heart, so is he."

Teddy Roosevelt claimed the formula for success is knowing how to get along with other people. Success is often determined by the way you treat others. Harsh people always reap harshness in their own lives. If you're not easy to get along with, you will not do very well in this life. A bad attitude will affect your career, your finances, and your relationships. Selfishness will leave you with what you love the most—yourself.

The Point of Living Is Giving and Loving

Don't allow a bad attitude to leave you stranded in the wilderness. The point of living is giving and loving. Deal with your baggage and change when necessary or you will be defeated.

Some attitudes may not seem to be positive, but they are because they are "Godward attitudes." Three Hebrew boys took a stand for God in Babylon and it brought serious trouble to their lives. When the King of Babylon warned them they would burn if they didn't bow to his golden image, those boys showed their "God-first-and-only" attitude:

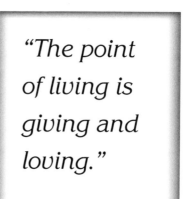

"The point of living is giving and loving."

> *If it be so*, our God whom we serve is able to deliver us from the furnace of blazing fire; and He will deliver us out of your hand, O king (Dan. 3:17).

The world may call that a bad attitude but God calls it a right attitude. This same right attitude has infuriated dictators, emperors, kings, and religious despots since the beginning of time.

If you put the Lord first, you can have that kind of attitude and stop worrying about your future, your kids, your business, your ministry, and your marriage. Put God first, and be willing to make changes when He commands it.

Yes, the enemy may hatch plots and schemes to destroy you and the things dear to you, but God will turn it all around for your good in His time. Take heart—if the enemy is fighting you, then you can be sure you must be going somewhere he doesn't want you to go.

Are you serving God first and only today? *If it be so*, then this too shall pass, and "...no weapon formed against you shall prosper" (see Is. 54:14). The right attitude sets the right altitude.

Receive Double For Your Trouble

If you are struggling through a low point today, hold onto your faith. The tide is about to turn and light is about to shine in your darkness. God is going to give you double for your trouble.

Over the years, I've worked with countless couples contemplating divorce. Healing and reconciliation is usually the result when both partners agree to seek God, honor His Word, and make a commitment to work things out.

When one of the partners refuses to seek counseling or reconciliation according to the principles in God's Word, the problems quickly multiply. Sometimes, one marriage partner will say, "I don't want to work things out—I just want out. I am going to do what I want to do, and I am going to live anyway I want to live."

Without exception, I have never seen the rebellious spouses succeed. Generally, they end up with nothing when it is all said and done. On the other hand, I've watched God bless the rejected spouses beyond their wildest dreams *when* they kept their hearts right and kept on serving.

Whether you face challenges in your personal life, finances, marriage, or ministry; keep your heart right and keep on serving God. He will bless you in the end. It may not come right when you feel it should come, but it *will come* at the perfect time in God's plan for your life.

The Answer Is Transformation

Hang onto your faith. If you are human, then you may wonder why God has allowed you to go through some of the difficulties in your life. This answer is transformation—God is *not* the author of the evil that comes your way, but He uses everything in life to change you into His image.

Attitudes Will Make You Or Break You

If your life seems to be "on hold" or under siege, then perhaps some changes are needed. Don't get mad at God. Examine yourself and start making the necessary changes.

God will not take you to a higher level until He changes and corrects dangerous weak areas in your life. Elijah the prophet did well on one level, but a new challenge (Jezebel) landed him alone and surviving beside a brook. Then everything dried up, and God took him to another place (see 1 Kings 17).

The prophet could have been angry with God and said, "God, I'm Your man. I am Your servant, so why did You let the brook dry up? Why did You stop sending the ravens to feed me?" The answer is that God let the brook dry up because He wanted Elijah to get up and move to another place.

When things dry up in your life, check your life for leaks, errors, disobedience, or changes that need to be made. Don't assume you need to change your location or divorce your spouse—look closer to home. What needs to change *in you*?

Hot Water Brings Out Your Flavor

Don't worry about being tested; it happens to everyone. It is in the test that God shows up in your life. He reveals just how big He really is when you pass through some hot water. Understand that you are basically a Kingdom teabag. *You have to go through some hot water before the flavor comes out.*

Attitude will make you or break you in times of trouble. When the Philistine giant, Goliath, taunted the armies of King Saul and the children of Israel, everyone was afraid of him. The universal opinion of the day was, "It is impossible to defeat this giant."

Young David the shepherd had a different attitude. When everyone else (including his brothers) said, "Man, he's too big to knock down"; David said, "No, he is too big to miss!"

David had an edge—he knew his God. He said, "Yea, though I walk through the valley of the shadow of death, I will fear no evil: for thou art with me; thy rod and thy staff they comfort me" (Ps. 23:4, KJV).

It is all about attitude.

Just because you have some failures in your life doesn't mean you are a failure. The Bible is full of people who failed yet became great—it was because God turned around their failures for their good and His glory.

David failed but God turned it around. Peter failed but God turned it around. Moses failed but God turned it around.

Failure is nothing more than a temporary set back. A right attitude will cause you to *grow* in the middle of your worst failure. You can't change where you have been or what you have done, but you *can* change where you are going and what you will do.

If you have had a bad attitude in the past, then make some changes today. Declare from your heart:

"I will obey God. This releases Him to command His blessing on me. I can't control the way people treat me, but I *will* control how I treat them, and what happens on the inside of me."

The difference between success and failure can be almost invisible or indiscernable. In World Olympics track contests, especially the 100-yard dash, the time differential between first place and last place may be only 1/10 of a second!

In the world of the heart, a bad attitude almost always ensures defeat. Your attitude will make you or break you. What kind of future do you desire? How high do you want to soar in your destiny? Do you want to hop like a grasshopper or fly like an eagle? Set your attitude today to match your desired altitude in Christ tomorrow!

(We are dedicated to serving you and God's kingdom in any way we can. Don't hesitate to contact us through our Internet website at www.DLministries.com).

Day 6

CHANGING FROM THE INSIDE OUT

One of the things I love about the Bible is that it was written by *imperfect people* who had made a lot of mistakes under the inspiration of our perfect and all-knowing God. Paul the apostle (a forgiven murderer) wrote:

> Brethren, I do not regard myself as having laid hold of it yet; but one thing I do: forgetting what lies behind and reaching forward to what lies ahead, I press on toward the goal for the prize of the upward call of God in Christ Jesus" (Phil. 3:13-14).

Paul the great apostle was saying in front of God and everybody else, "I haven't arrived yet. I am still learning and changing." What if he refused to change? What a shame to go through life and you discover that you keep making the same mistakes over and over.

When you meet people with addictive behaviors, you will probably discover that one of their "roots" is bad. Something extreme causes them to go out all the way in everything that they do. They don't do anything part way. Why? Their addictions help make them feel good temporarily.

Addictions don't go away on their own. You have to go to the hidden *root* of the addiction problem to deal with the visible harvest of problems it produces. It is the same regardless of the addiction—alcohol, drugs, tobacco, illicit sex, or the acquisition of extreme power or money. There is a root at the base of every human addiction that must be dealt with. *You can't deal with the fruit until you deal with the root!*

> ## "God's Word possesses the power to change you from the inside out."

The Book of Joshua declares: "This book of the law shall not depart from your mouth, but you shall meditate on it day and night, so that you may be careful to do according to all that is written in it; for then you will make your way prosperous, and then you will have success" (Josh. 1:8). The New Testament tells us why:

> For the word of God is living and active and sharper than any two-edged sword, and piercing as far as the division of soul and spirit, of both joints and marrow, and able to judge the thoughts and intentions of the heart (Heb. 4:12).

God's Word Possesses the Power to Change You

Unlike a new pair of shoes, a new car, or a new job title, *God's Word possesses the power to change you from the inside out.* It does more than merely change the way you look on the exterior—it fundamentally changes your spirit and moves outward transforming your soul, your mind, your emotions, your body, and your outward actions!

People who don't feel good about themselves tend to develop addictive or obsessive behaviors. Some people eat to feel better about themselves. Others get high on drugs or alcohol, or indulge in sexual sins for the same purpose.

Addictions are simply outward fruit of what is operating inside a person's soul. God's Word is more powerful than all of our tendencies, failures, appetites, or fears.

What does it mean to "change from the inside out"? It involves more than merely modifying your behavior; it is about changing the condition of your heart. *If you just modify your behavior then you will revert back to it all the time.* It springs from the heart-felt prayer: "God change me from the inside out."

This is a process of changing the heart—not just the head or a learned habit. The process begins the moment you bare your soul to the Lord and pray:

"God I see sin, failure, weakness, and unbelief in myself. I need help. I am asking You to strengthen me, guide me, and change me. Lord God, I pour myself out before You. I lay my life on the altar as a living sacrifice. I need You. Work on me from the inside out and make me pleasing in Your sight."

Does Your Heart Harden or Soften In Times of Trouble?

You do not have to go from one negative cycle of failure to the next. Let me ask you a question: "Is your heart soft like wax that has been exposed to heat? Or is your heart like modeling clay that *hardens* when exposed to heat?"

Some people experience a softening of the heart when they go through trouble. They begin to say, "God, I see it. I am sorry, Lord. Please forgive me and change me."

Other people become hard-hearted in times of trouble. The more trouble comes their way, the harder their hearts become. They also tend to become harder to get along with than other people. It is a heart thing.

Make an attitude correction. Make a heart change. "God, change me from the inside out; cause me to become soft when You speak to me or correct me."

If you want to be a success in life, then you may have to go against your personality at times. God doesn't give any of us an "exemption" to His commands.

His Word commands us to love one another and *act loving* as well (see Mt. 22:37-39, 1 Cor. 13). You may think that you don't have a "friendly" personality, but God commands that you love your brother. That marks the end of the discussion and the end of all excuses. Just be loving.

The Bible says give and it shall be given back to us, so whatever we give determines what will come back to us—irregardless of any special circumstances or exemptions we claim to have (see Lk. 6:38).

If you have a bad attitude, the first thing you must do is change what you are saying. Your words are like the rudder or steering mechanism of a ship—they will guide you to a good or a bad attitude.

I Couldn't See the Other Side From There

Attitude is very similar to altitude where the heart is concerned. During a ministry trip to New York City, my hosts told me that New Jersey was just across the river, but when I looked in the direction they pointed I couldn't see the other side from there.

"Well, it's not very far, it's just right over there," they said. No matter how hard I looked, I still couldn't see it. Then we boarded an airplane and by the time we had climbed about 200 feet above the ground, I could see New Jersey exactly where my friends said it was.

The point is that I had to climb higher than where I was to see what I was needed to see. Sometimes you have got to climb higher using the vehicle of your words. By lining up your words with God's Word, He will take you higher than the way you presently act or treat people. Then you will see and act the way God tells you to act.

You can't control the way people treat you, but you can totally control the way *you* treat them. Before I was saved, I used to "go off" in anger or disgust toward people whom I felt deserved it. Now I exhibit the fruit of the Spirit—specifically, the fruit of self-control—toward others because Christ lives within me.

With God's help, I can control my attitude now and it has changed the way I treat people. Genuine change begins on the inside.

Your Attitude Determines Your Altitude

Your future is not determined by what happens to you, or even by what you do outwardly. Your future is determined by what happens on the inside of you. Your attitude determines your altitude, and your faith in the Lord determines your progress tomorrow.

If you are still breathing and the Spirit of God dwells inside of you, then I guarantee that you are on God's potter's wheel. It is His way of helping you learn how to change. It is only through the process of change that you become what He has called you to be.

It is on the potter's wheel that the Potter deals with the flaws and disfiguring events of the *past.* This is important because the past directly influences the way we respond to people or situations each day. Our behavior is directly affected by the roots of our lives, for good or for evil. God requires us to examine the roots in our lives—it is the only way we can produce good fruit.

> *"You can't control the way people treat you, but you can totally control the way you treat them."*

When we get hurt, it is human nature to build walls around our wounds. Ideally, the walls come down after the wounds heal, but in practical terms, we just keep building those walls higher and thicker. We just keep on building walls and fortifying the old ones until we block out people and God Himself.

None of us are perfect. We raise our kids imperfectly, teaching them to raise their kids imperfectly, and so the dysfunction is passed on from generation to generation. This is exactly why God requires you to honestly examine and evaluate your life.

You Must Expose Your Wounds Before Jesus Will Heal Them

We want to hide every wound, disfigurement, and flaw. Jesus commands us to expose them before He will heal them. Jesus told one man in a public meeting:

> And He said to the man with the withered hand, *"Rise and come forward!"*...He said to the man, *"Stretch out your hand."* And he stretched it out, and his hand was restored (Mk. 3:3,5).

If you have a wound or a hidden flaw in your life, don't hide it. Stretch it out to God right now. You can't fix the thing on your own, and there is no benefit to hiding it any longer. Ask Him to help you. Admit to the Lord that only He can fix the problem, and then allow Him to take care of it for you!

Understand that flaws and all, God never stops loving you. He doesn't love you "because of who you are"; He loves you because of who He is.

Even when you blow it, He still loves you. He doesn't condone your sin and excuses, but He always loves you. If He can forgive you, then surely you can forgive yourself.

When you gave your life to Him, you became the righteousness of God in Christ. You may not look like it at the moment. Perhaps you didn't act like it yesterday. Nevertheless God says, "By faith I call you My righteous." I am the righteousness of God. That means He loves me.

The enemy works desperately to make you think that God is mad at you because *love is the very thing that will heal you.* God's unconditional love is the very thing that will break the negative cycles you fall into time after time.

Remember that God's love is based upon who He is, not upon who you are and what you can do. When you obey Him, He blesses you. When I disobey Him, there are consequences to pay. Nevertheless, His love for you never changes or ends.

God isn't mad at you. Now forgive yourself. God isn't holding your failures against you. You can afford to start liking yourself.

Do you think of yourself as too young, too old, too black or too white? Do you believe that you are more than a conqueror, or do you believe that you are victim? Let God's Word on the matter change you from the inside out.

Exchange the enemy's spirit of heaviness for God's garment of praise! Make a strategic attitude correction and climb a little higher. If

46

you have suffered some setbacks in life, then understand this: *With God involved, every setback becomes an opportunity for a comeback!*

(Change is not always easy, but it is inevitable. If we can help you or pray for you, don't hesitate to contact us through our Internet website at www.DLministries.com).

Day 7

BREAKING NEGATIVE CYCLES

Either make the tree good, and its fruit good; or make
the tree bad, and its fruit bad; for the tree is known by
its fruit (Mt. 12:33).

Your future is intimately intertwined with the things hidden in your
heart. Are those things good or bad, negative or positive? Your
answer closely resembles your future.

Even if you feel as if you are camped outside hell's gate right now, I
have good news for you: You do not have to go from one negative cycle
to the next! The Lord is ready to help you, but true change doesn't start
from the outside. Godly change starts from within.

You can't always take a straight line driving from one city to the
next. You may need to jog left or right, speed up, or slow down. That
is the way life is.

We all have to make adjustments when we run into disappointments, difficulties, and failures in life. Sometimes we even have to
make a u-turn.

If you want something you don't have, then be prepared to do something you have never done. It is *not* too late to turn around things.

Anyone who refuses to deal with the hurts in their heart will struggle with negativity and inferiority. They tend to go through life convinced that *everybody else* is the problem. (It is easier to blame others than look honestly at yourself.)

Let God heal your hurts. People with hurting hearts rarely change or grow up on their own, and hurting people hurt other people.

Jesus assured us we would know what is inside a person by looking at the fruit they produce. Negative fruit is a telltale sign of a spiritual heart problem. Jesus said, "You brood of vipers, how can you, being evil, speak what is good? *For the mouth speaks out of that which fills the heart*" (Mt. 12:34).

Many Christians bounce from one broken relationship to the next, from job to job, from city to city, and even from church to church. These negative cycles constantly produce fresh pain.

Let Jesus Break That Vicious Cycle

Your patterns of negativity may trace all the way back to your childhood years, but the bottom line is that Jesus can help you break free of that vicious cycle. He came to give you an abundant life and bless your finances, your marriage, your children, your emotions, and every other area of your life (see Jn. 10:10).

Once you allow the Lord to heal your heart and break its negative cycles, then nothing can hold you down or hold you back. The Bible says, "Watch over your heart with all diligence, for from it flow *the springs of life*" (Pr. 4:23). Open your heart and open the flow of God's power in your life!

A medical "wellness check" begins with an examination and honest evaluation. A spiritual "heart check" begins the same way. What kind of fruit is being produced in your life? Is there joy? Is there self-control? Is there peace in your heart?

Hearts that are broken, wounded, and *left untended* tend to produce gossip, bitterness, anger, pride, and unforgiveness. Give your hurts and wounds to God and obey His Word. Don't wait on other people to repent or ask for forgiveness. Forgive, release others, and speak only loving words about other people. This releases blessings to you.

People who feel abandoned or rejected struggle to develop healthy relationships because they are trapped in perpetually negative cycles. They are so desperate for love that they often squeeze the life out of people around them, and they tend to fear true commitment. Deal with these wounds through Christ or they will entrap you for life.

We Are Good At Finding "Things" to Hide Our Pain

By "dealing with wounds and hurts," I am *not* talking about covering them up or temporarily blocking the pain. We are good at finding "things"

> *"We are good at finding "things" to hide or ease our pain for short periods of time..."*

to hide or ease our pain for short periods of time—our temporary fixes include food, drinks (especially alcoholic drinks), drugs, new clothes and adult "toys" such as cars and houses.

Our basements and attics are full of unused workout machines, athletic equipment, and sports gear that we bought on guilt or pain splurges. We buy the stuff and then put it in the nearest corner where it sits for a year (then we move it to the attic to make room for even newer useless gear).

Health clubs tend to be profitable today, but I'm convinced it is *not* because so many people join them and *use them*. It seems that many of people who sign those membership contracts and pay monthly payments rarely use the facilities!

Jesus gave us three simple steps to heal our hurting hearts, drawn from the Old Testament. He said the two greatest commandments in the Bible were to love the Lord your God with all your heart and to love your neighbor as yourself (my paraphrase of Mt. 22:37-40).

The first step to your healing is to love God with all of your heart. Religion won't heal you; it will make you worse. Only a genuine relationship with God will heal your wounds and help you overcome the issues in your heart.

I thank God for counselors, but the best counselors ultimately lead you to the Word of God and the God of the Word. Even successful secular counselors bring healing primarily by following biblical principles (whether they know it or not).

All human beings have an inborn emptiness in their hearts, and we are all looking for something to fill that emptiness. Some turn to drugs, others seek satisfaction in booze, sex, money, or power. Until you have a relationship with the Lord that emptiness will remain. No matter what you try, none of it will satisfy until you surrender all to God and love Him with all of your heart.

The second step to your healing is to love your neighbor. When you get hurt or wounded in your heart, do you tend to isolate yourself and become loner? As long as you remain a loner you will not see healing come into your heart. Many suicide victims are loners who probably would *not* have killed themselves had they been connected to other people.

Even though the Lord begins to fill our emptiness when we come to Him, we have to learn how to connect with other people. Loving and supportive relationships with other people make it easier to change and be healed.

By God's design, *you need people*. It is His plan for us to be healed and stay whole through life-giving relationships in His church, the body of Christ. The more you love God the more He puts His love in your heart for other people.

Years ago, I really didn't like being around people. I grew up in church and didn't like it, so when I got old enough to walk away I did. Then I went out into the world and found myself a pigpen with other prodigal sons.

When I came to the Lord, I was grateful just to be saved. God began the process of changing me and it hurt, but I was glad the darkness was out of my life. Then I was gently coerced into teaching Bible studies. I didn't really like it but I did it anyway and one thing led to another.

Breaking Negative Cycles

Our home Bible study grew so much that we had to move to a storefront space, and then we had to build a big building. I didn't want to do any of it because I was a businessman, not a preacher. I still consider myself a businessman teaching God's principles for building houses from the foundation up.

I said, "Lord, You know I'm a business man. I'm not a preacher, and I don't even like people. God, I don't want to be a preacher, but it looks like You are going to make me do it." The Lord said, "Son, you can walk away any time you want to. I gave you a free will, so if you don't want to do it, don't do it." And that is when I said, "I'm sorry Lord." Once God calls you, you can't be happy doing anything else.

Then God began to work in my heart so I could see people through His eyes and love them the way He loves them. Today, I love people so much that I will lay down my life for them as a true shepherd lays down his life for his sheep.

God will do for you what He has done for me. Simply lower your guard and take off your mask. Tell Him, "Lord, I need to be changed." He will complete the good work He has begun in your life (Phil. 1:6).

The Bible says, "If someone says, 'I love God,' and hates his brother, he is a liar; for the one who does not love his brother whom he has seen, cannot love God whom he has not seen" (1 Jn. 4:20).

Some people are so negative that they are untouchable. It is as if they wear a sign that says, "Don't touch me!" They aren't bad people; they are wounded and fearful people who live in the dangerous realm of "negative faith." They have *faith* that the worst things possible will happen in their relationships with others. Unfortunately, negative faith produces a bumper crop of negative fruit.

Love your neighbor and enjoy the healthy fruit of loving, supportive relationships.

Step number three to your healing is to love yourself. First you love God with all of your heart. Second, you begin to connect with people and share life with them. Third, you must love yourself—complete with all of your imperfections. Stop being so hard on yourself. Sometimes, you can be your own worst enemy! Change the words that you say about yourself.

Ask God to forgive you for your sins and shortcomings. Understand that He puts it under the blood of Christ where it is removed forever. If God can forgive you, surely you can forgive yourself.

If you love God with all your heart, He will begin to work in your heart. Every new day in Christ brings new strength and love into your life from the inside out. One day you will notice that you really love those people you didn't have time for earlier. Once you love God and love people, you will begin to accept yourself and love yourself for who you are.

A healthy heart produces good fruit. A whole and complete heart produces a successful life, a happy marriage, and blessed children. Are you satisfied with the fruit in your life? Would you like to see the fruit change?

> *"Understand that change is a process, not an event."*

The Apostle Paul said the "fruit" or outward evidence of an evil or negative heart includes things like immorality, impurity, sensuality, sorcery, jealousy, outbursts of anger; fighting, envy and drunkenness (see Gal. 5:19-21).

People know the Spirit is in your heart when they see these things in you: love, joy, peace, patience, kindness, goodness, faithfulness, gentleness, and self-control (see Gal. 5:22-23).

Most of us aren't "there" yet, so we have some changing to do with God's help. Understand that *change is a process, not an event.* It is a whole string of things that happen over a long period of time.

When I gave my life to the Lord, He launched a process that began to change me (it is still going on). If you could have seen me "before Christ," then you would *know* there is a mighty God in heaven. I am *not* the man I once was—I am a better man in Christ!

I learned that you can come to church seven days a week *without changing*. You will not change until you get God's Word in your heart. Treat the Bible as you do the food you eat every day—you *have* to take it in to live. Meditate on it; speak it out of your own heart. If you don't, you will never receive complete healing or lasting change.

Breaking Negative Cycles

The Apostle Paul said God's Word "... is living and active and sharper than any two-edged sword, and piercing as far as the division of soul and spirit, of both joints and marrow, and able to judge the thoughts and intentions of the heart" (Heb. 4:12b). Do you want to overcome the issues in your life? Get God's Word in your heart.

When the brokenness and wounded places in your heart are healed, everything around you will change. Once your heart is whole, your life will begin to change.

Remember that the words of your mouth reveal the "abundance of your heart." When you hear doubt and unbelief coming out of your mouth; then realize your negativity is showing.

Repent and pray:

> "Lord, change me. I'm dealing with the issues in my heart. Do a new work in me. I will love You will all of my heart, soul, and might; and I will reprogram my heart and mind with Your Word. Help me to love others the way You love them."

(If you are struggling to break negative cycles in your life or ministry but feel you need some help, don't hesitate to contact us through our Internet website at www.DLministries.com).

Day 8

CHANGING A NEGATIVE MIND

Worry and fear just seem to come naturally to adult human beings, but it seems extremely unnatural in children.

Do we basically *teach* our children how to worry and fear things? I know that we have to *work* at overcoming these things as adults. Faith and trust in God don't seem to come naturally for us.

Isn't it odd that we have to *practice* praying with thanksgiving when we have so much to be thankful for? It seems much more "natural" to complain or whine to God than to thank Him for what He has done and is doing. What does the Bible say?

> Be anxious [worried and negative] for nothing, but in everything by prayer and supplication with thanksgiving let your requests be made known to God. And the peace of God, which surpasses all comprehension, *shall guard your hearts and your minds* in Christ Jesus (Phil. 4:6-7).

57

If God's peace *guards* our hearts and minds; that must mean they *need to be guarded from something!* The mind is a great battlefield and our enemy is focused on making us wander off into the no-man's land of fear, worry, and negative thinking.

The "accuser of the brethren" has spent thousands of years learning to influence human behavior with floods of negativity each day. The Bible says, "Be of sober spirit, be on the alert. Your adversary, the devil, prowls about like a roaring lion, seeking someone to devour. But *resist him, firm in your faith...*" (1 Pet. 5:8-9a).

Negative thinking produces many of the problems we deal with each day, but faith in God and His Word overturns and reverses it all. Paul said "we wrestle not with flesh and blood but powers of darkness." Understand as a believer that this war is not about people—it is about spiritual powers and the battle of the mind.

The Violent and Vital Fight Over Your Mind

God commands us in strong language to take control of our thoughts. This reveals just how violent and vital the fight over your mind really is:

> ...for the weapons of our warfare are not of the flesh, but divinely powerful for the destruction of fortresses. We are *destroying speculations* and every lofty thing raised up against the knowledge of God, and we are *taking every thought captive* to the obedience of Christ (2 Cor. 10:4-5).

The enemy bombards your mind with cruise missiles labeled "nagging thoughts and fears." Paul calls them "fiery darts" (KJV) or "flaming missiles" (NASB) in Ephesians 6:16. Ralph Waldo Emerson said, "Everything begins with a thought." A far wiser man named Solomon said, "As he thinketh in his heart, so is he." Is your life is off track? Check your thinking.

Paul's prescribed cure for negativity was a thought life focused on good things:

Finally, brethren, whatever is true, whatever is honorable, whatever is right, whatever is pure, whatever is lovely, whatever is of good repute, if there is any excellence and if anything worthy of praise, *let your mind dwell on these things.* The things you have learned and received and heard and seen in me, *practice* these things; and the God of peace shall be with you (Phil. 4:8-9).

The enemy is happiest when God's people think negatively and live in discouragement without joy or any hope for the future. He can steal everything that we have at that point.

Most people go through life buried in negative thoughts, but successful people learn to think positively. Jesus said, "In the world you have tribulation, but take courage; I have overcome the world" (John 16:33b). Give God your problems and never accept a quitter's mentality.

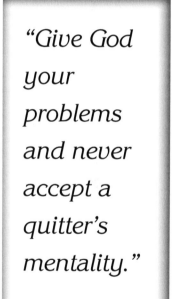

"Give God your problems and never accept a quitter's mentality."

Be Transformed from a Negative to a Positive Thinker

God will take you through the storm. Don't quit. Do something to change your thinking and your life. Allow His Word to transform you from a negative to a positive thinker. Find out what *God* says about you and live it out as Jesus did. Don't confront wrong thinking with earthly weapons or skillful arguments. Run to the battle armed with His Word, the Name of Jesus, and the power of the Holy Ghost.

Jump off the roller coaster of a life controlled by emotions. Stand on what God says about your situation. Negative thoughts produce negative words, which produce a negative life. A negative outlook on life is totally incompatible with the walk of faith in God.

Your mind is in a war—a continual war. The natural mind opposes the things of the Spirit. You cannot succeed on your job or in marriage harboring a negative thought life.

I don't believe you can see your life straightened out until you get your thinking straightened out. Everyone may pray for you, you may feel goose bumps on your goose bumps, but you will be in even worse shape tomorrow if you fail to change your thought life.

Good thinking may not guarantee success, but it will certainly improve your chances for success. When negative or fearful thoughts come in, tell yourself, "No, I am not going there." Get into God's Word and meditate on what He says about life and destiny.

Some Folks Never Succeed Because
They Have Stinking Thinking

We all have great potential in Christ. He doesn't love one color or size better than others. Since thinking helps shape who you are, you need good thinking to reach your potential. Some folks never succeed because they have stinking thinking.

Make changes in the way you think if you want to change the way you live. Bad attitudes spring up from negative thinking and good attitudes come from good thinking.

Failure is not the end, but negative thinking just might take you there. Discover God's plans for your life and stop receiving what the devil has planned for your life. Exchange that "stinkin' thinkin'" for the godly thinking promised to you when you received "the mind of Christ" (see 1 Cor. 2:16).

Set goals and reach for them. Negative thinking won't get you there, so make some changes *now*.

It doesn't matter whether you are 6 or 106 years old, you need to make changes in your life to help you find success in Christ. The Bible says, "And do not be conformed to this world, but *be transformed by the renewing of your mind*, that you may prove what the will of God is..." (Rom. 12:2a).

Get renewed with the Word. Be in Church every time the doors open, pray fervently, and get your thinking turned around.

Changing a Negative Mind

Never go by your feelings if you have decided to obey God. Your feelings will tell you one thing while the Word says something else. We are in a perpetual war on this earth, and the devil is *still* "a liar and the father of lies" (see Jn. 8:44).

Trust God, Never Steer By Your Circumstances

Jesus came to bring you the abundant life. Where you are today is not where you're going to stay. Make the decision right now to change your negative thinking and trust God, never steer by your circumstances.

God did not create you to be a failure. It's only a matter of time until God turns things around, but don't be offended by trouble or persecution. The Bible says, "And indeed, all who desire to live godly in Christ Jesus will be persecuted" (2 Tim. 3:12).

Jesus didn't come to remove all opposition; He gave us all the tools we need to overcome in this life.

You have been down and out and going in circles long enough. Change is a catalyst for growth. Embrace God's change so He can lift you out of the rut and get you moving in a new direction.

Before I gave my life to the Lord, I had the nagging thought that I was going to die at an early age. I felt that some catastrophe, car wreck or tragedy would kill me at an early age. Two times I was struck by cars as a child, and perhaps this explains how negative thought were embedded in me from an early age.

As an adult, I had more New Year's resolutions than I could remember, but I could not change myself. Now I know that the enemy was trying to control my thought life. I was immersed in a war over my mind, and somehow I turned to God's Word and I began to confess *His* plans and destiny over my life. Positive changes soon followed.

I began to confess principles from God's Word:

The enemy is lying to me, because God has a plan for my life, it is for good and not for evil, and it is for a future, not an early death. No weapon formed against me shall prosper. I can't go under because I am going over (see Jn. 8:44, Jer. 29:11, Isa. 54:17, Deut. 28:1-13).

Somewhere along the way I got a hold of the Word of God and I began to say, "*I can't lose with the Word of God that I use!*" This could be your year for a breakthrough if you learn how to change your negative thinking into Christ-like thinking. You will come out of this thing if you walk away from negative thinking.

Failure is not the end, but you can see it standing on the mountain of negativity. Change your view, change your position, and enjoy divine provision. Remember: You are in a war over your mind. Someone is going to win and someone is going to lose. The decision is yours.

(If you are committed to changing the way you think, live, and serve God, we would like to help if possible. We are dedicated to serving you and God's kingdom in any way we can. Don't hesitate to contact us through our Internet website at www.DLministries.com).

Day 9

WHY IS MY LIFE ON HOLD?

Is your life on hold? Do you see people around you getting blessed and wonder why God's Word doesn't seem to be working for you? After preparing for the ministry, are you still waiting (and hating it)? Are you still believing God for a spouse and wondering why you haven't had a date in years? You are probably wondering, Why is my life on hold?

> Trust in the Lord, and do good; dwell in the land and cultivate faithfulness. Delight yourself in the Lord; and He will give you the desires of your heart... Rest in the Lord and wait patiently for Him; do not fret because of him who prospers in his way, because of the man who carries out wicked schemes...The steps of a man are established by the Lord (Ps. 37:3-4,7, 23a).

The steps of a good person are ordered by God; so we must have faith that we will walk into the promises of God as long as we walk with Him. Even if your steps lead you into a storm, you will eventually walk out of your trouble.

Samuel anointed young David to be king of Israel, but many years passed before he was finally crowned as king. God led him through the wilderness and had him live in caves. People talked about him, armies chased him, Saul took away his wife and gave her to another man, and David even spent some time in jail because he wasn't ready (see 1 Sam. 16—2 Sam. 5:4).

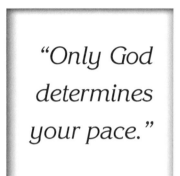

"Only God determines your pace."

When God begins to move in your life, He will allow you to go through some "stuff" to change you and take you to where He wants you to go. Sometimes it happens quickly and sometimes it doesn't. Your heavenly Father knows best.

It took 17 years for David to move from the pasture to the palace, but it was only because he wasn't ready. As for God, He is "sitting on ready."

After God knocked Saul of Tarsus off his donkey, he was born-again and started preaching the gospel immediately. Whether you are on the fast track or the slow lane, if you love the Lord, you must entrust your life to His hands.

God Will Make You Fearless and Faithful

The enemy wants you to be fearful and doubtful, but God will make you fearless and faithful. He is in charge of your life and He is ordering your steps. Trust Him to work things out in your life. When your mind says nothing is working out and all is lost, God says, "All is found because I Am." Who will you believe?

Only God determines your pace. Your job is to be faithful, no matter what you're going through. You may think you are ready for that spouse or ministry you've asked for, but if you grasp at them before your time, you may destroy what God ordained for you!

When the master potter takes the clay, he takes it and molds it into the image he wants it to be. Once he molds it, it's just a piece of raw pottery. It's been molded but it hasn't been set in the fire yet.

Why Is My Life on Hold?

A master potter molds the clay into the desired shape and gently places the pottery in a kiln or intensely hot oven. The purpose of the fire is to temper the clay so it will withstand pressure once it is pulled out of the furnace. If you give your life to the Lord, the Master Potter will mold you, and then gently place you in the fire.

You may not like that kind of preaching or teaching, but true life in Christ is never a bed of roses (although it is *always* worth it). If you skip the fire, you will break very easily. All true disciples have pressures come against them (see 2 Tim. 3:12). You must withstand a lot of pressure to make it to the end of this race.

A lot of people may start a marathon, but only the persistent actually cross the finish line. The life of a disciple is not a 100-yard dash for personal glory; it is a marathon for endurance. When you've been in the fire, a new strength arises inside you. "Wait a minute—I've already gone through hell and high water, now I *know* no weapon formed against me is going to prosper."

Out of the Furnace and Onto God's Shelf

Once a potter pulls his pottery out of the furnace, he sets the pottery on a cooling shelf for a while. If He pulls it out of the fire and uses it too quickly, it will crack. When God pulls you out of the furnace, He will set you on a shelf for a time. He doesn't want you to be like the people who gave their lives to the Lord and too quickly started preaching and stepping into the spotlight on public platforms. If they start thinking they are something they are not, they will crack and collapse under the pressure.

"God, I am ready for my husband now; I've been through the fire."

"No, I have placed you on a shelf to let you cure for a little while."

"God, I am ready for my ministry. Bring it on, baby."

"No, I have to let you sit for a while. I have to move you to a place where you are praying and trusting me totally every day."

Fear will make you believe God is not going to use you. Remember that God has promised you that *in due season* you would reap your harvest *if* you don't grow weary (see Gal. 6:9). God has you on a shelf to cure and mature for a little while. He has you on hold for a divine purpose, and He hasn't forgotten about you. He is letting you age and mature before He really uses you.

God has you on hold to deal with some lingering bad attitudes. Perhaps you are still too controlling—He can't give you authority until that flaw is worked or baked out of you. Perhaps He is waiting for you to take the mask off. "Yes Lord, I'm arrogant and prideful. I need Your help. I still have that jealousy problem. God I take off the mask."

Joseph was a young boy who had a dream that all of his family members would one day bow before him. He foolishly started telling them, "You are going to bow to me before this is over."

God Wasn't Angry, He Prepared Joseph to Rule and Reign

I can imagine God saying, "Boy, I want to use you but I must send you into slavery for a while. First you will go to prison for 12 years in a foreign land." God wasn't angry with Joseph; He was preparing him to rule and to reign. He had to break Joseph's arrogance and pride, and He taught him to be faithful.

Joseph became faithful during those dozen years in Pharaoh's dungeon. Sometimes God must change your surroundings to get your attention. Joseph didn't realize until later that God had his life on hold because He was preparing him to be promoted (see Gen. 45:5-8).

God is preparing you for something great. He put you on hold for a reason—He is out to capture your attention and work out some things hidden within you. He wants you to quit compromising and decide to go all the way.

If your life is on hold, the chances are good that God is trying to make changes in you. Don't get mad at God. Learn to say yes instead of no. None of us like to wait; we are ready to go now. The problem is that if you don't have enough spiritual strength in your life, you won't make it.

You can blame the preacher, your mama, your ex, your boss, the white man, the black man, or everybody except yourself—but nothing will happen until you take off the mask and say, "Okay God, I'm ready for change."

Learn to Walk By Faith and Not By Sight

Your life is on hold because God wants you to change. Submit to the will of God and He will see that you get where you need to go.

Why Is My Life on Hold?

Don't get frustrated because people are getting blessed more than you are or because things seem to be moving too slowly in your life. It is all part of learning to walk by faith and not by sight.

Feelings will fool you and they may destroy you. Read God's Word and know what He says. If you live by feelings you will never pay your tithes and end up living in lack. Feelings will tell you to never forgive anyone who hurts you. Faith will help you forgive.

God will take your life off of hold when you have learned what you need to learn. Meanwhile, cast all your cares on the Lord because He cares for you (1 Pet. 5:7). If you find yourself in a fiery furnace, know that God is working out some things in your life. He protects and teaches you in the process of changing you. You may be on hold today, but God is taking you somewhere.

When the Lord says it is your season, then nothing can stop you. It is darkest just before the dawn. The enemy will attack you most aggressively just before your victory. If your life is on hold, if you feel as if you are in the fire; it is because God wants you to be tempered. He wants you to come out of that fire with some spiritual strength and stamina. He wants to form you into a fine piece of china instead of an old clay pot.

Your life will stay on hold until you say, "Lord, I give You my problem. Change me." Don't get impatient, it may lead you to make a wrong decision with painful consequences. God is never late because He knows the end from the beginning. He knows what it will take to get you ready, so pray this prayer with me:

> Father God, change me. Do something new in me. Forgive me of my sins as I forgive those who have sinned against me. I have been hurt, but I know You can heal me.

> Reveal Your perfect will for me as I humble myself before You and surrender my body as a living sacrifice. I open up my heart to hear what You have to say. I understand that I must change if my life is to get off of hold. Not my will but Thy will be done.

(We are dedicated to serving you and God's kingdom in any way we can. Don't hesitate to contact us through our Internet website at www.DLministries.com).

Day 10

ANGER MANAGEMENT

Why are we so angry?

We all have anger issues, but some of us just seem to hide them better than others. The triggers that ignite your anger may be different from those that light another person's fire, but the triggers are there.

What are the hidden "hot spots" of sensitivity in your life?

- When people don't do what is right.

- When a friend betrays you.

- When your expectations aren't met.

- When a spouse leaves you—and leaves you penniless with a whole pile of bills.

When you are born again, you lay aside the old ways and put on the new self in Christ (see 2 Cor. 5:17). Where we used to think it was acceptable to explode in anger at people, now we know we must deal with our anger correctly. Otherwise, we might give a place to the enemy in our lives (Eph. 4:26-27).

Nearly everyone gets angry about something once in a while, but some people live at a *perpetual boil*. They hope they can keep one step ahead of a stroke or heart attack.

Others send their anger "underground" into the soul, essentially sweeping everything under the carpet where it begins to eat away at body and soul around the clock. Some simply drug themselves into oblivion to escape their anger, while other just keep building walls.

Whenever I read about Moses' ministry, I have to wonder: *What if Moses had dealt with his anger* when he killed the Egyptian? If his anger had been under control, perhaps he wouldn't have hit the rock, the action that barred him from the Promised Land! (see Num. 20:8-12) The moral of the story is, "If you will deal with your anger now, it will save you a whole lot of mess in the future.

> *"No matter what others do to us, we must take responsibility and deal with our issues".*

No matter what others do to us, we must take responsibility and deal with our issues. It is not a sin to be angry *unless* your anger causes you to be out of control. Jesus was angry with the religious folk who opposed Him, but He did not sin.

James told us to be ... "slow to speak and slow to anger" (Jas. 1:19b). Most of us are quick to talk and quick to be angry.

Anger can be a byproduct of suffering, injustice, betrayal, persecution, prejudice, broken promises, unmet expectations, or even righteous correction. We all deal with anger in different ways.

I Refuse to See You or Speak to You

Some people *avoid* the people or things that anger them. Others give people the silent treatment, using mood swings to influence or control people around them.

Anger Management

God says, "Be angry, and yet do not sin; do not let the sun go down on your anger, and do not give the devil an opportunity" (Eph. 4:26-27).

Many people who were raised by a controlling parent or parents have a difficult time with control issues, and they often become controlling themselves. This is a form of witchcraft, because it is all about power and control through self-will and the manipulation of others. If you try to control people you will hurt them, even if you have the best of intentions.

Anger hinders relationships, pushes people away, and endangers marriage relationships. Many times anger explodes over very small or inconsequential irritations—why would grown adults quarrel over toilet lids, socks on the floor, or the dishes in the sink? When we don't feel loved we become angry.

Uncontrolled anger produces devastating results. That's why you have to be very careful how you discipline your children. Never "discipline" them by withdrawing your love. Discipline your children in love.

Time Bombs Ready to Explode

Our jails and prisons are full of people who lost control of their anger. Many people today are *time bombs ready to explode.* With all of the stress and pressure in our lives, we all feel as if we will explode at one time or another.

Paul said to *put away all anger.* Since you have given your life to the Lord, you are responsible for the way you deal with people, for your actions, and how you deal with the wounded areas of your life.

The very process of living creates pressure in our lives. We face financial pressures, pressure on the job, plus the usual family pressures of raising children and helping rebellious or restless teens through adolescence. Then we face the pressures of illness, accidents, and unexpected problems. Life can be a pressure cooker sometimes.

Anger flashes out when people are overlooked because of their color or gender; or when parents unwisely favor one child over another. Some things are just not worth hanging onto. God even said that He would make it up to you if you had enough faith and let it go and just trust in Him.

Maybe you are angry because you think that God has let you down. Maybe you are angry because you put your faith in the Lord and He did not come through the way you thought He would. Anytime you are disappointed in God, anger will try to rise up in you.

The only way you will ever control your anger is through an intimate relationship with the Lord Himself. You must dive deep into God's Word and discover what God says about it. *Begin a life of prayer and* examination, and avoid pride at all costs.

Samson Had a Serious Anger and Rebellion Problem

Samson was one of the greatest judges or deliverers in Israel's history, but he had a serious anger and rebellion problem. Because his anger was out of control, he was feared but not respected.

He chose to ignore the warnings of his parents and of God Himself and married a woman who did not serve God. In anger, he killed 30 men for their clothes just to pay off a bet concerning his new bride.

Samson thought that he could live his life any way he wanted without paying the consequences, and many Christians today seem to feel the same way.

Later on, Samson became so jealous that anger overtook him again. He caught 300 foxes and tied their tails together in pairs and attached torches to them. They ran through the fields of the Philistines and destroyed them in flames (see Judg. 14-15).

When the Philistines found out what Samson had done, they killed his wife and her father by burning them alive. What a tragedy! It was all because Samson's anger got away from him.

Samson had a pattern or believing that *he could handle anything.* He thought he could play with and taunt the enemy and never be defeated. I wonder how many people in the church think they can play with the crack pipe or date unsaved people and not be defeated?

Men, in general, are notorious for thinking they can handle anything. If they are not careful, the pressures build until they explode.

When that happens, we unknowingly push everybody away and create an atmosphere of disrespect.

You Can Defuse Any Time Bomb

Some people are walking time bombs because they have been hurt and don't know how to deal with their issues from the past. With God's help, you *can* defuse any time bomb before it is too late. If you do not learn to go to God with your pressures, you could end up exploding and hurting the people closest to you.

Depression is a national epidemic in America, affecting even the very young. If you continually suffer from depression, look for evidence of *unresolved anger* in your life. Anytime you suffer from depression, you can be almost certain there will be some kind of conflict in your life that you must deal with.

Prozac seems to be the national drug of choice among the clinically depressed. Unfortunately, most of these people are merely medicating the issues. Medication does not and cannot solve spiritual issues of the heart.

> *You must take off the mask if you want to overcome anger issues in your life.*

The key to healing is being able to admit there are some deep issues causing the depression. "I may not know what they are, but I have to get to the root of this thing so I can get out of this pit."

You must take off the mask if you want to overcome anger issues in your life. Quit living in denial. You must overcome your short fuse and admit you need God's help. You have to make some changes. James the apostle said, "Confess your sins to one another, and pray for one another, so that you may be healed" (Jas. 5:16).

Healthy relationships are built around respect and trust. How can you respect somebody who loses control of his temper? It is time for us to learn to communicate about our feelings openly, but not in anger or harshness.

Get To the Heart of Your Hurts

This principle applies even if you came from an abusive family, where anger seemed to rule your entire house. Get to the heart of the things that have hurt you. Put your pride aside and begin to deal with those sensitive issues. Remember: "A gentle answer turns away wrath, but a harsh word stirs up anger" (Pr. 15:1).

Above all, *quit blaming others* for your anger. Take responsibility for yourself and repent. *You* can break the cycle of anger, control, and jealousy in your life—but you can't do it by yourself. This is your prescription: "I can do all things through [Christ] who strengthens me" (Phil. 4:13).

Go to the Lord in prayer and ask Him to give you the grace to forgive everyone who controlled or hurt you. He will give you the grace to forgive people you thought you could never forgive!

Quit looking at yourself as a victim. Perhaps it is true that *before* you gave your life to the Lord, you were a victim. However, *now* you are *more than a conqueror!* You are in the process of overcoming the pain of your past and resolving those issues. Let it go.

Anger management is directly related to your walk with the Lord. Victory comes as you say, "God, here it is. I need Your help and I need Your strength. I can do all things through Christ who strengthens me."

Get rooted in the love of God and things will change.

Admit you are angry; then stop and ask yourself, "What am I angry about? Where did this anger come from? What is the root cause of this?"

Anger is a fruit that grows from something that is rooted inside of you. Get in a right relationship with the Lord and you will be able to manage your anger.

Walk step by step with me through the Apostle Paul's formula for peace and joy in the church:

Anger Management

> Let no unwholesome word proceed from your mouth,
> but only such a word as is good for edification...
> (Eph. 4:29a).

That means we should avoid any form of backbiting, murmuring, or gossip and cursing. "Edification" means "to build up." That defines the only kind of words that you should be speaking.

> ... according to the need of the moment, that it may
> give grace to those who hear. And do not grieve the
> Holy Spirit of God, by whom you were sealed for the
> day of redemption (Eph. 4:29b-30).

In other words, you will grieve the Holy Spirit by murmuring, backbiting, and being critical of other people.

> Let all bitterness and wrath and anger and clamor and
> slander be put away from you, along with all malice
> (Eph. 4:31).

In other words, you are to put away anger. Never let it stay or linger in your heart or life, then you won't have to worry that it will pour out in the form of bitterness or slander.

> And be kind to one another... (Eph. 4:32a).

Don't be mean. Don't be judgmental. Don't be harsh. Don't be demanding. Don't be overpowering. Don't be too aggressive or pushy. Be kind, as you would want people to act toward you. The apostle's final statement needs no further explanation:

> ...tender-hearted, forgiving each other, just as God in
> Christ also has forgiven you (Eph. 4:32b).

(If you feel anger is still getting the best of you, perhaps we can help. Don't hesitate to contact us through our Internet website at www.DLministries.com).

Day 11

A ROOT OF BITTERNESS

> ...let us also lay aside *every encumbrance*, and the sin which so easily entangles us, and let us run with endurance the race that is set before us...
>
> Pursue peace with all men, and the sanctification without which no one will see the Lord. See to it that no one comes short of the grace of God; that no *root of bitterness* springing up causes trouble, and by it many be defiled; (Heb. 12:1, 14-15).

You have an in-your-face, up-close-and-personal enemy who is totally sold out and dedicated to place a root of rejection, bitterness and anger inside your soul. This ancient evil spirit especially delights in warping the young. His plan is to bring so many anger-laden entanglements into our lives that unhappiness hovers over us day and night.

People who live with anger around the clock can't seem to help themselves. They know they need to be around other people, but they push or drive people away so effectively that they often live lonely, isolated lives.

Their anger has moved inward to form what the Bible calls a root of bitterness in their souls. A root of bitterness is to the spirit of man what cancer is to the body.

Satan's plan from the beginning of your life was to injure you so deeply that he could plant a root of bitterness inside you. He is skillful at using a root of bitterness to control you through anger.

Paul told us to lay aside every hindrance, every issue that would try to entangle us. When we come to the Lord, we all come to the Lord with entanglements. Some of us have ropes, chains, and webs wrapped around us almost to our noses. We must look like Lazarus moments after he hobbled out of the tomb, wrapped up like a mummy in grave clothes.

Jesus Issued a Second Command: Loose Him!

Technically, Lazarus was alive. But in reality, he was so bound up that Jesus had to issue a *second command* so he could begin to act, look, and live like he was alive. "And he that was dead came forth, *bound hand and foot with graveclothes*: and his face was bound about with a napkin. Jesus saith unto them, *Loose him*, and *let him go* (Jn. 11:44, KJV).

No one who is normal really *wants* to be hurt. This explains why we expend so much effort building protective walls with the building blocks of our low self-esteem, anger, and bitterness. We do it because we are tired of being hurt by other people.

When you are so bound up that all other people see are your "graveclothes," most folks will avoid you out of fear. They won't tell you the truth about how bad you look, they will just turn away. This feeds another bitter response from you: "I'm tired of them treating me like that." In this way, the bitter cycle of isolation and loneliness just keeps getting worse.

If you want me to point out your graveclothes problem, then I can help you. You are bound-up and entangled by whatever causes you to lose control. It happens over and over, year after year. You just can't seem to let go of it or win release from it.

A Root of Bitterness

Another clue is found in your words. What do you shout, complain, or warn people about the most? Controlling people usually stand up and shout to everyone else, "You are *not* going to control me!" Critical people point their fingers at other folks and say, "Your problem is that you are too critical. Haven't you ever read what the Bible says about a plank in the eye?"

You know you have a root of bitterness in your life when no one can correct you. You are so sensitive to what you view as rejection in any corrective comment, that you immediately—almost instinctively—become angry. What makes you red-hot? Is it criticism of your body, of your educational level, or your parents?

Bitterness Takes Root In Sinners And Saints

The root of bitterness has no favorites—it shows up in sinner and saint alike. You can be saved, sanctified, and filled with the Holy Ghost...but be so bitter that you still push people away through your pain.

Anger causes people to operate out of their emotions rather than operating out of the Word of God.

> "You can be saved, sanctified and filled with the Holy Ghost... but be so bitter that you still push people away through your pain."

Angry Christians who have not won freedom through the truth of the cross quickly lose control when they think of the times people said they were no good, ugly, or stupid.

Men seem to have more anger issues even than women, perhaps because women are taught to release their emotions while men are taught to be "tough." The bottom line is we all grew up with rejection and anger issues. Now it is time to begin the process of examination. I can't tell you what your issues are—that is your job.

When you go to a garden or vegetable patch to pull weeds, sometimes you have to uncover the root. You push aside all of the distracting debris and you spread apart the deceiving upper foliage. A root is something you can't see on the surface. It goes deeper than what you can see.

If you "pull a weed" from the top, then all you come away with are the green leafy tops in your hands. The root remains to reproduce again, only bigger, better, and more hardy. We go for the root for a reason: It is the only way to kill the thing and destroy its power to reproduce.

Examine your life for bitter roots stemming from painful family relationships—are you at genuine peace with your father and mother, with your sisters or brothers, and with your other family members?

Search Out Every Bitter Memory

You have to search out every painful memory before you can deal with them. Search your heart for every bitter memory of rejection by schoolmates, friends, organizations, or leaders. Do those memories still possess the power to trigger anger in your soul—even though the memory dates back several decades in your life?

You can tell someone they are beautiful over and over again, but if they are suffering from the bitter root of rejection, then they can't receive or believe your words. My wife and I went to a restaurant recently and a very beautiful young lady came to wait on our table. We instantly realized that she had an inferiority complex. I told my wife, "Honey, that girl has no idea how beautiful she is."

You know there is a root of anger inside you when:

1. You yell because you are frustrated. ("Well Pastor, that's just the way we were in my family." I know, my family was the same way. But that doesn't make it right.)

2. You hit or strike out when you are angry. (I am talking about all hitting—a man hitting a woman, a woman hitting a man, adults hitting children or pets. If it happens in any form, then you have an anger problem.)

A Root of Bitterness

3. You find that you are attracted to people who have the same problems with anger and rage that you do. (I can tell you what you think of yourself by your friends because birds of a feather flock together. The truth is that sick people attract sick people, which only perpetuates our mess even more.)

4. You don't like yourself and you don't like anybody else either.

5. You're a controller. You try to control who your spouse's friends are.

6. If you have a hard time trusting.

Failure is not the end of your life, your marriage, your ministry, or your career. But if you don't probe deeper to discover how you reached the point of failure, you might end up at that very same point again. This is especially true for the root of anger or bitterness. Discovery, honesty, repentance, and forgiveness through Jesus Christ—this is the only cure.

It is time to break the cycle of anger and bitterness in your life.

(Bitterness can be a formidable enemy, but you can overcome it. Don't hesitate to contact us for help or prayer through our Internet website at www.DLministries.com).

Day 12

DO I HAVE TO FORGIVE YOU AGAIN?

Jesus said, "Truly I say to you, whatever you shall bind on earth shall be bound in heaven. Whatever you shall loose on earth shall be loosed in heaven. Again I say to you that if two of you agree on earth about anything that they may ask it shall be done for them by my father who is in heaven. Where any two or three are gathered in my name, there I am in their midst." Then Peter came and said to him, "Lord how often shall my brothers sin against me and I forgive him? Up to seven times?" (Mt. 18:18-21).

Jewish law required observant Jews to forgive three times a day. So Peter thought he was really going the extra mile when he suggested that the amount be stretched out to seven times in one day.

Jesus said to him, "I do not say to you, up to seven times, but up to seventy times seven" (Mt. 18:22).

83

Even on our best days, with the best of intentions, we may do things that hurt others. If we quickly repent and make amends, things might go along just fine.

Unfortunately, most of us talk as if "everyone else" is the problem and we make excuses for our issues. We stubbornly cling to the idea that we are justified in our anger and unforgiveness toward others.

Human nature says, "Hold grudges, get an attitude and press charges against those that hurt us." When we grow up in Christ, we learn to forgive and release things.

> *"The nature of God is to bless us in spite of what we do"*

Stop Being Childish

Spiritual maturity is measured by how we put away childish things (such as unforgiveness and resentment). How well do you release things when you get hurt?

> When I was a child, I used to speak as a child. I used to think as a child, I used reason as a child. But now that I am growing up I've become a man in Christ. Now I learn to put away those childish things (adapted from 1 Cor. 13:11).

The nature of God is to bless us in spite of what we do. The entire gospel message is about forgiveness. God isn't mad at you; He wants to heal you, help you, and restore your life!

God's principles are very simple: "Whatever I give out is what I get back, whether it is meanness, love, forgiveness, or judgmental attitudes" (see Lk. 6:38). Did you realize that one of satan's greatest weapons against you are your own hurt feelings?

The good news is that if I don't hold anything against you, then God won't hold anything against me! The measure that I give to you is the measure that God makes sure is given back to me. That is why I *have* to be a giver.

Do I Have to Forgive You Again?

Jesus prayed, "Our Father who art in heaven, hallowed be Thy name. Thy kingdom come. Thy will be done, on earth as it is in heaven. Give us this day our daily bread. And forgive us our debts, as we also have forgiven our debtors" (Mt. 6:9-12).

Even your forgiveness depends in part on your ability and willingness to forgive others. If people have hurt you, Jesus said to forgive them as you have been forgiven. It doesn't even do any good to ask for forgiveness unless you are forgiving others at the same time.

If you forgive a spoonful, then you will be forgiven a spoonful. Forgive a scoop full and you are forgiven a scoop full. I don't know about you, but I need a lot of forgiveness. If I forgive you a shovel full, I'm going to get the same kind of forgiveness back to me. If I forgive you a wheelbarrow full....

If you can't receive forgiveness, it is probably because you won't release people from the things they've done to you! *Do I have to forgive you again?* Well, it depends. Do you want to be forgiven yourself?

Do I Have to Forgive Them Again?

"But Pastor, they asked me for forgiveness and they turned right around and did the *same* thing again. Do I have to forgive them again?" It depends on what you want in your own life.

Some people pray and pray, and they ask, "God, forgive me for what I've done." However, they don't ever feel forgiven. They know they asked for forgiveness but their emotions don't let them feel forgiven. That is because they wouldn't release others from offense, and now they cannot find release themselves.

You must reach a point where you can look at the person that's hurt you and say, "I forgive you. I let it go. I release you of all your debts, and I let it go now." May I say that some things are just not worth hanging on to.

You see, if I forgive you a little bit, then I am forgiven a little bit. If I totally release you of what you've done, then I can be totally released from what I've done.

It's like in marriage. As long as you are praying, "Lord, change *that woman* I am married to," then not much is going to change in your life. You should pray, "Lord, change *me*. God, make *me* what You want me to be."

Pray "Lord, Change Me"

Even if the other parties are all wrong and you are all right, the prayer has to be, "Lord, change me."

Forgive everybody in your past, just in case you need some forgiveness in the future. Quit hanging onto unforgiveness. It is a liability. I don't care what the grievance is. It keeps you from going where God wants you to go.

> *"Forgiveness is all about releasing others."*

Jesus said, "Whatever you bind on earth shall be bound in heaven. Whatever you shall loose on earth shall be loosed in heaven" (Mt. 16:19). If you read through several verses in Matthew 16, notice the context.

Did you notice that the context was not about demons? The context was forgiveness. Whatever I bind on earth is bound in heaven. In other words, when I hold you hostage on earth, I'm held hostage in heaven. When I release you on earth, I'm released in the heavens.

Forgiveness is all about releasing others. It is more than merely saying some words; it is the action of letting someone off the hook, of releasing them.

May I say it another way? *Whatever you hold against others, God will hold against you.* Whatever you release others from, God will release you from.

One of satan's favorite weapons may be the guilt and condemnation he brings into our lives. When you have forgiven others, the enemy is powerless to hold you hostage. The Bible commands us to "give no place to the devil" (Eph. 4:27). When you don't let things go, you give place to the devil to come into your life.

Sometimes you have to forgive an ex-husband so you can get along with your current husband! Sometimes you have to forgive those in your past so you can have some kind of a future. When something stinks in the refrigerator, you pull out everything and find what it is that stinks. If something is stinking in your life right now, quit blaming everyone else and begin to pull everything out one by one.

Jesus said, "If you don't forgive others from your heart, your heavenly Father won't forgive you." If you refuse to forgive others for what they've done, your heavenly Father will not forgive you. In my book, *Don't Judge My Future By My Past*, I talk about getting your past behind you once and for all. Just because you failed in the past doesn't mean that God is through with you (Contact DLministries.com for more information).

Hell Is Full of the Self-Justified

It doesn't matter if you feel *justified* in why you hate the person who hurt you. Hell is full of the self-justified, people who felt justified over their decision not to let an offense go.

"Do I have to forgive you *again* for what you've done to me?" It depends. Do you want to go to hell or heaven?

Anytime you refuse to release others from the wrongs they have done to you, you have essentially placed handcuffs on God—He can't do anything for you. God cannot answer certain prayers until you take the handcuffs off of Him through your forgiveness.

When you don't forgive people for the things they've done, the one you hurt the most is yourself. In fact, if you don't let go of the things that have happened, you may actually bring a curse back on yourself! You don't get advancements on your job. Your money becomes less. You have no friends. Unforgiveness is an ugly thing.

We all feel justified in our anger, but the problem is that it holds us hostage and forces us to live behind walls of bitterness. Yes, offenses may come your way but you have too much living to do and too many places to go to hold on to that anger.

"But Pastor, how do you forgive somebody who has destroyed your family? How do you forgive someone who has stolen your childhood?" Jesus said, "Pray for those that abuse you." As you begin to pray, God begins to do a work in you.

When I choose to obey God, I put myself in a position to receive everything that God has for me. When I release you, I put myself in a position to be released and blessed by God! Man can help you, but not like God can.

Tormenters are released in your life anytime you don't forgive others. Anytime you don't forgive others, you open the door for hell to come against you.

Why do ships sink? Because "the stuff on the outside gets on the inside." Why do people fail? Because all the bitterness and pain on the outside was allowed to come inside. Failure is not the end if you will forgive people and let go of the past.

Some things aren't worth hanging on to. Sometimes you just have to let go and say, "Lord forgive me from my sins, as I forgive those who have sinned against me."

(Some people seem to push us to the edge where forgiveness is concerned. We are dedicated to serving you as you serve God's purposes. Don't hesitate to contact us through our Internet website at www.DLministries.com).

Day 13

FORGIVING UNDESERVING PEOPLE

> Truly I say to you, whoever says to this mountain, "Be taken up and cast into the sea," and does not doubt in his heart, but believes that what he says is going to happen, it shall be granted him. Therefore I say to you, all things for which you pray and ask, believe that you have received them, and they shall be granted you. And whenever you stand praying, forgive, if you have anything against anyone; so that your Father also who is in heaven may forgive you your transgressions. But if you do not forgive, neither will your Father who is in heaven forgive your transgressions (Mk. 11:23-26).

If you belong to the Lord, He says that you can talk to the mountains in your life. This is a Kingdom principle that applies to every area of life. You can talk to your problems and command them to move if you believe in your heart that God can do anything.

This principle is especially important when dealing with the biggest mountain blocking many Christians from their destiny in Christ—the mountain of offense.

God has demonstrated through His Son and the Cross that He forgives people who do not deserve to be forgiven. Why are we surprised that He expects us to do the same thing?

He expects us to walk in forgiveness whether or not we feel it. It is not optional; it is a command. If you want to be everything God called you to be, you must be quick to forgive and faithful to reconcile.

Jesus said, "...whenever you stand praying, forgive" (Mk. 11:25). If you don't forgive others, your Heavenly Father won't forgive you. If you forgive, mountains will move. If you don't, your mountains will not move.

Obviously, God takes forgiveness very seriously. He makes it plain that if you don't forgive, then He won't forgive you! That is blunt and painfully clear—God is making a point we had better receive. Honestly, you may end up in hell if you insist on holding onto unforgiveness in your heart!

Reach Out and Forgive

The sin nature is selfish, controlling, critical, and extremely unforgiving. The new man we become in Christ is exactly the opposite. We have an anointing from God to reach out to and forgive people who do not deserve to be forgiven.

The outward sins of the flesh such as drugs, sexual sin, and drunkenness are obviously wrong and we love to talk about them (because most of us find it easy to avoid them). However, *none of these sins are as serious as unforgiveness* in the eyes of God.

When you decide not to forgive someone else, you are in big trouble with God. Those mountains will not move for you. Miracles will not happen, nor will the financial breakthroughs you may need so urgently.

God gives you the fruit of what you honor and worship the most—the fruit of selfishness and unforgiveness or the fruit of the Spirit. Nothing good comes to you when you cling to your personal issues and bitterness against others.

Forgiving Undeserving People

Stop everything and take a good look at yourself. You will never change unless you become uncomfortable enough with your sinful unforgiveness. Strip off every mask and examine yourself with brutal honesty.

This may be the most important point in the kingdom of God: You might make it to heaven with all kinds of failures in your life, but *you may not make it if you hang onto unforgiveness* in your heart.

You Didn't Deserve To Be Forgiven Either!

Unforgiveness is the very nature of satan; forgiveness is the nature of God. Now that you are born again, God expects you to forgive. He expects you to forgive people that don't deserve to be forgiven. After all, *you didn't deserve to be forgiven* either!

If you have been abused, you must trust God to help you *forgive the abuser.* Otherwise you will stay wounded all of your life. The Greater One lives inside you now with an anointing to forgive people who don't deserve to be forgiven.

God said to Israel, "If ye be willing and obedient, ye shall eat the good of the land: But if ye refuse and rebel, ye shall be devoured..." (Isa. 1:19-20a, KJV).

> *"You will continue to struggle under a spirit of failure unless you do things God's way."*

If you have nothing but leftovers in your life, look closely at yourself and quit blaming other people. You will continue to struggle under a spirit of failure unless you do things God's way.

Anytime you get your feelings hurt, you must decide: "I will release this person, it is my privilege," or "I will hang onto my offense—it is my right."

If your temper rises when you think about someone, it shows you still have an attitude about that person and you haven't let it go. It is all about growing up in Christ to full maturity. It is easy to forgive people who are loving and only occasionally hurt people unintentionally. God wants us to walk in forgiveness toward *everyone—even the jerks.*

When I was a baby Christian (understand that you can be saved fifty years and still be a baby Christian), I used to get an attitude when I got hurt. Now that I've grown up in Christ, I try to make the decision quickly, "I will let it go." You will stay wounded all your life until you learn to forgive and let go of issues.

Spiritual Babies Are All About "Me, Me, Me"

How many know that babies are all about, "me, me, me?" "I want you to change my diaper. I want you to hold me. I...I...I will make your life miserable until you do what I tell you to do." .

Baby Christians are like that. "I've got to get my needs met." "What's the Church going to do for me?" "What am I going to get out of this, Pastor?" It's all about me.

God's kingdom is exactly the opposite. Forgetting about me and beginning to sow into other people's lives and beginning to help other people.

I'll even go so far as to tell you that unforgiveness is nothing more than baggage. You know, all baggage is a liability. What is your net worth? Assets minus liabilities is your net worth. What is your net worth? Are you bankrupt or are you blessed? Because all baggage is a liability. If you've got more baggage than you've got assets, you've got negative net worth. Folk may love you but you've got so much baggage they can't stand to be with you. You're bankrupt.

Christians like to say, "Well, I'll forgive you but I'm not going to forget it." Lord, forgive us. It's our way of holding people hostage for the things they've done to us. The problem is that *we* are the ones who become the hostages. We become emotionally bankrupt.

Unforgiveness ties you to the person that hurt you. When I don't forgive you, I've got to think about you all the time. I don't even want to be in the same room with you and I've got to think about you all the time. If I've got unforgiveness in my heart, I'm tied to you with an invisible cord that I've got to drag around everywhere I go. Night or day, It's not worth it. Let it go.

Sometimes you have to say, "I am hurting, but I will let it go. I don't like where I am, but I will let it go. I can't carry you all of my life. I'm going to let this thing go.

Jesus said that unless you become like a child you cannot enter the kingdom of heaven. What did He mean by that statement? A child, when they get hurt, they just let it go. Even when they get hurt, they just let it go. Unless we become like a child, we cannot enter the kingdom of heaven.

Jesus told a story in Matthew 18. He said that a certain king had a slave that owed him millions of dollars. Because the man had no way of repaying the debt, the king forgave him for what he owed.

But the same slave that had been forgiven of the debt had a friend that owed him just a few dollars. He grabbed his friend and told him "Repay the money or else I'm going to have you thrown in prison."

The king heard what the slave did. So he went to him and said, "I forgave you of an impossible debt that you couldn't repay. But you wouldn't forgive others, and because you wouldn't forgive them now I'm going to make you pay." The way you forgive others is the way God forgives you. The way you release others is the way God releases you.

Jesus said, "My Heavenly Father will do the same thing to you if you don't forgive your fellow man from your heart. Your debt was so great against heaven that there was no way you could have repaid it and God forgave you, and now you have got to forgive people of an impossible debt."

The Unforgiving Will Be Turned Over to Tormentors

Jesus said that if you don't forgive others, you will be turned over to the tormenters. Unforgiveness will cause you to lose sleep and be hateful. It will eat at your insides and cause you to live under a spirit of failure. Stop and look at your life.

As we noted earlier, you must forgive others if you expect God to forgive, heal, or deliver you. "Give, and it will be given to you; good measure, pressed down, shaken together, running over, they will pour into your lap. For by your standard of measure it will be measured to you in return" (Lk. 6:38). The way you give determines the way you receive.

Forgiveness requires humility because the only true way to forgive is to lower yourself. Some people are so full of pride that they can't even see the unforgiveness in their heart. Pride says, "They're not going to do this to me. They've talked about me long enough." Don't shift blame, or you will stay just like you are the rest of your life.

You always reap what you sow. The person who can't forgive others can't even forgive themselves. Bitterness is nothing more than a faith issue. *It takes faith to forgive* and release people who have hurt you. Jesus gives us no choice on the matter.

> If therefore you are presenting your offering at the altar, and there remember that your brother has something against you, leave your offering there before the altar, and go your way; first be reconciled to your brother, and then come and present your offering (Mt. 5:23).

Go To Those You Have Offended

God doesn't even want your money as long as you have bitterness in your heart. If you know someone has been offended by you, then go to them and try to bring healing to the situation. Not everybody will accept it, but you can get it out of your heart.

Faith works by love, so if you don't forgive others, your faith won't work. Maybe that's why some folk never see a miracle.

Jesus was abused and mistreated, beaten mercilessly and spit upon, ridiculed and nailed to a rugged cross. Yet, He cried out from the depths of His heart, "Father, forgive them for they know not what they do" (see Lk. 23:34).

God wants you to forgive and release people—even when they don't deserve it. Your miracle may depend on what you do with this message.

Make no mistake; we don't forgive people because they deserve it. We forgive them because we are commanded to forgive them.

Forgiving Undeserving People

God's way is to forgive undeserving people, and He has called us to be like Him.

(The truth is that none of us deserve to be forgiven, but it is still difficult forgiving difficult people at times. Don't hesitate to contact us if we can help or pray. Visit our Internet website at www.DLministries.com).

Day 14

THAT WAS THEN,
BUT THIS IS NOW

Then the Egyptians chased after them with all the horses and chariots of Pharaoh, his horsemen and his army, and they overtook them camping by the sea...

...But Moses said to the people, "Do not fear! Stand by and see the salvation of the LORD which He will accomplish for you today; for the Egyptians whom you have seen today, you will never see them again forever.

...So Moses stretched out his hand over the sea, and the sea returned to its normal state at daybreak, while the Egyptians were fleeing right into it; then the LORD overthrew the Egyptians in the midst of the sea. And the waters returned and covered the chariots and the horsemen, even Pharaoh's entire army that had gone into the sea after them; not even one of them remained (Ex. 14:9, 13, 27-28).

I have failed in the past and my past has been chasing me, but it's over.

That was then and this is now.

No matter who you are, you have skeletons in your closet and things in your past that you would like to forget. One voice in the universe is dedicated to reminding you of your failures every moment of your existence. God's Word calls this enemy "the accuser of the brethren," and for good reason (see Rev. 12:10). He loves to take your past and throw it in your face.

The enemy haunts your present with images and voices of the past because he wants to stop your progress in the Lord. Where the Lord convicts of sin to bring freedom, your enemy condemns with sin to bring bondage.

The Bible says there is no condemnation or condemning sentence for those that are in Christ Jesus (see Rom. 8:1). Yes you failed, but that was then and this is now. Failure isn't the end. In Christ, it marks the beginning of a glorious new life!

The enemy of your soul is determined to pull you back into the things of your past. That means that even *after* you get saved, the enemy will tempt you, threaten you, and harass you in an attempt to pull you back into the very things God delivered you from!

The Sins of Your Past Will Follow You Into the Present

If you give in to your enemy, the very sins you were involved in before you were reborn *will actually follow you into the church!* Don't let the sins of your past follow you into the present! You would be surprised how much sexual sin, drug activity, and unrestrained pride is in the church of Jesus Christ.

It seems as though after we are born again, our past truly chases us even harder than usual for a while. This explains why so many young Christians have such a struggle with issues in the past.

The enemy will use the past to steal your future—if you allow it. By holding you to your past, he hopes to steal the purpose and destiny God ordained for you in your life.

That Was Then, But This Is Now

The children of Israel were delivered from Egypt's Pharaoh, but even as they prepared to cross into a new chapter of their lives...the past came charging up behind them to captivate them again.

God told them to *stand their ground* and *face their past once and for all*. When they obeyed, they watched while God destroyed and forever buried the captors of their past for them.

Are you so ashamed of your past that you avoid any mention of it? It is time to face yesterday's sins and bondage once and for all so God can destroy it. The devil wants you to feel guilt and shame for the rest of your life so you will never enter into the promises of God.

> *"Face your past and watch God destroy it by the blood of Jesus Christ."*

Face your past and watch God destroy it by the blood of Jesus Christ. The children of Israel escaped through the Red Sea—you and I receive freedom through the sea of blood Jesus Christ shed on Calvary. It washes away and buries your sins once and for all. What are you running from? Who are you running from?

There Is No Condemning Sentence For Those In Christ

The Bible says you are the righteousness of God in Christ (see 2 Cor. 5:21b). You are covered in his righteousness and there is no condemning sentence for those that are in Christ Jesus.

Your enemy is desperate to pull you back to the past *because you are going somewhere*. He is trying to stop your destiny. I am happy to tell you that God isn't looking for perfect people (there are none). He is looking for repentant people who know who they are in Christ.

Isn't it amazing how God will talk to you about your future when everything looks dark and hopeless? You may feel weak and defeated yet He will call you a mighty man of valor! Remember: He calls things that be not as though they were.

Only God will talk to you about your future when the enemy is telling you that you have blown it! God talks to you about where you are going instead of where you are.

Let go of the things in the past so God can do a new thing in your life! Rise up and possess the land. Get up again and fight the good fight of faith. Don't sit there and say, "Oh, God, why don't you help me?" Get up and fight back! God says it is yours, but you have to go after it!

It is time to cross over into the promises of God and bury the past. It's time to let go of the past.

Bury Your Past or Your Past Will Bury You

If your past is chasing you or calling you back, then you are at a crossroads today. You must know who you are in Christ before you move forward and cross over into your future. Sometimes you have to look back at your past and say, "I'm through with it. Dust to dust and ashes to ashes." Either you bury your past at the cross or your past will bury you under a false weight of guilt and condemnation.

The next time someone tries to condemn and sentence you to your past, open your mouth and say, "That was then, but this is now!" When someone tells you that God would never use someone like you, open your mouth and say, "That was then, but this is now. Yes, I used to do those things, but the old me is dead. I have been reborn. That was then and this is now."

We have all failed and fall short of His glory. We all have weak areas in our lives that tend to cause us to fail. But just because you have failed in the past does not mean you will fail in the future. That was then and this is now. Things have changed because Jesus Christ lives in your heart—you are the righteousness of God.

God's mercies are new every morning. He has mercy for every kind of failure. He has mercy for forgiveness of sin and for healing your body. He has mercy to heal your broken heart and to lift you out of every bondage in your life!

I Don't Have to Worry About God Being Mad At Me

David said, "Surely goodness and mercy will follow me all the days of my life, and I will dwell in the house of the Lord forever" (Ps.

23:6). Even when I make a mistake, I don't have to worry about God being mad at me.

Paul said, "Let us therefore come boldly unto the throne of grace, that we may obtain mercy, and find grace to help in time of need" (Heb. 4:16). Anytime we need something from God, we can boldly crawl up in His lap and say, "Daddy, I need Your forgiveness. Daddy, I messed up, I need Your help."

Any time we surrender to the Lord, He promises to have compassion on us and remember our sins no more (see Micah 7:19). The enemy does just the opposite, but his opinions and claims don't matter. He keeps digging up your sins and throwing them in your face, so you have to say, "My sins are in the past and covered by the blood of the Lamb. They are gone!"

You don't have to be perfect for God to use you or bless you. Keep a soft and repentant heart, and don't let the enemy steal your faith! God blesses those who love Him.

The Bible says, "Eye hath not seen, nor ear heard, neither have entered into the heart of man, the things which God hath prepared for them that love him" (1 Cor. 2:9, KJV).

I can predict your future if Jesus Christ is your Lord and Savior (and it won't cost $3.99 per minute either). Oh, I've got it: "Surely, goodness and mercy are going to follow you all the days of your life and you shall dwell in the house of the Lord forever" (see Ps. 23:6). Aren't you glad that the blood of Jesus has covered up your past? Even better than covering it up, the blood of the Lamb completely wiped it out!

Don't tell me where I've been—I've already been there! Tell me about my future. Tell me where I'm going in the Lord. Tell me what He will do for me if I love Him, but don't judge me by my past.

I know I've made some mistakes in the past, but I have learned from my failures and I am not going to make the same mistakes again! I am going somewhere with my life because God loves me and He is working on me. The work He began in me, He will perfect until the day of Christ Jesus.

This is the Good News: You can overcome all the shame, all the accusations, by the Blood of the Lamb and the word of your testimony! Declare this proclamation with me:

I testify that my sins are under the blood. I testify that His blood covered up my past. I testify that that was then and this is now.

(It is vital that you move from "then" to "now" in God. We are dedicated to helping you in any way we can. Don't hesitate to contact us through our Internet website at www.DLministries.com).

Day 15

BEING A GOOD MONEY MANAGER

> For it is just like a man about to go on a journey, who called his own slaves, and entrusted his possessions to them. And to one he gave five talents, to another, two, and to another, one, each according to his own ability; and he went on his journey (Mt. 25:14-15).

A wealthy man entrusted his possessions to his servants before going away on a journey. He understood what many in America do not—people are different, and so are their abilities.

The Lord's Parable of the Talents is a familiar one. It is a story of great success and of failure that *was* the end of one man's career. Above all, this story contains vital keys to being a good steward over your finances.

According to Jesus, this wealthy master gave one especially able servant five talents (think "bags of gold"). A second servant received two talents, and the third received one talent (and we soon learn why).

The first servant *immediately* began to invest the money and soon doubled it. The second servant also went to work quickly and also doubled the money.

Both of these servants were told, "Well done, good and faithful slave; you were faithful with a few things, I will put you in charge of many things, enter into the joy of your master" (Mt. 25:21, 23).

The third servant buried the money he had. When his master asked about his results, the servant revealed his ignorance and arrogance through the sad view he held of his master.

> "Master, I knew you to be a hard man, reaping where
> you did not sow, and gathering where you scattered
> no seed. And I was afraid…" (Mt. 25:24-25).

This man *began* by shifting blame to the master! He said he reaped where he didn't sow and gathered where he scattered no seed. (Some people today still try to blame God for their financial woes.)

More Interested In Excuses Than In Excelling

It seems this servant forgot—as many of us do today—that the *seed* (or capital) came from his master. As a slave, *he* was assigned the task of producing something with the master's seed money. He was more interested in excuses than in excelling to please his master. (The devil is a liar—so don't join him by making excuses instead of excelling.)

Your success may depend on your ability to learn from this man's failure thousands of years ago. He was afraid—probably because his character flaws and poor performance gave him good reason to be afraid. Your enemy wants to keep *you* afraid and at a distance from God so you won't receive any more than what you already have. This is the master's heated response:

> You wicked, lazy slave, you knew that I reap where I
> did not sow, and gather where I scattered no seed.
> Then you ought to have put my money in the bank,
> and on my arrival I would have received my money
> back with interest. Therefore take away the talent

from him, and give it to the one who has the ten talents (Mt. 25:26-28).

God never tells you to work what you don't have; he never asks you to give what you don't have. However, he does expect you to be faithful with what you have.

One reason we tithe is because we can't let money become our God. As long as we faithfully give God the first 10 percent, then we can be positive that the "money god" won't get a hold of us.

Do Your Best With What You Have

If you want to get your finances in order, then you can't be afraid. Put God first and work diligently with what is at hand. You may not have as much money or the same abilities as the person next to you, but you can do your best with what you have.

> *"The #1 cause of divorce in America is money."*

Jesus said the servant who did nothing with little was wicked and lazy. Be a good steward over the little things so God can *trust* you with the big things.

The enemy, on the other hand, works against your mind constantly. He says, "You don't have enough. You can't give like Mr. So and So. You'll end up with no food for your kids." It is a lie. If you have *something*, then you can always tithe on it. The enemy just doesn't want you to enter the joy and abundant blessings of the Master.

If you spend more than you bring in, then you need to make some changes. God isn't focused on how much money you make, He watches how you manage what you have.

The #1 cause of divorce in America is money. Improper money management causes tremendous stress in marriages and families because it always produces excessive debt. Debt *equals* bondage and most Americans are in bondage because we have a problem with what the Bible calls "the lust of the eyes." We want everything and we want it now.

Corporate America capitalizes on our compulsive lust of the eyes. Lenders send a flood of unsolicited credit cards to young people the moment they enter college or a vo-tech school. (By the way, if you don't pay off your credit card *in full* each month, you have *excessive debt.*)

As long as you're in debt you will never have true prosperity, and the enemy will use that debt to convince you that you "can't afford" to tithe in obedience to the Word. God says the tithe is His. It is a command, not an option.

Make the Tithe Your First Check

How do you obey the command to tithe if you are already in debt? Make your tithe the *first check* you write after a deposit. Be faithful to put God first in your finances, or it may be hard or biblically impossible for Him to bless you.

The Bible says that when you tithe, God Himself *rebukes the devourer* for your sake! (see Malachi 3). When you don't tithe, He can't rebuke the devourer. When you give an offering, God will multiply the seed back to you. When you are saddled with excessive debt, how can you possibly give offerings above the tithe?

Quit fighting over money and follow this simple pattern: *Write the plan, then work the plan.* Warning: It may involve making some cuts, getting a second job, or making some sacrifices for a while, but no one excels or succeeds without making sacrifices.

The cornerstone of financial freedom is a good and reasonable budget or "spending guideline." The budget may be your most important tool for getting out of debt bondage and creating wealth for your family, for your children, for your grandchildren.

Six Steps to Building a Budget

1. Write down your goals. Are you trying to get out of debt? What is your purpose in setting a budget. Are you trying to clear up your credit?

2. Determine your monthly income, include all sources of income, but always determine your net income.

3. Determine all your monthly expenses. Go back and look in your checkbook to see what they are because a lot of times you forget.

4. Subtract all the expenses from the net income.

5. Determine all other expenses, like dining out, dry cleaning, babysitters, etc.

6. Determine what you can do to reach your goals.

Take what you have now and build a budget based on real expenditures in the past. If you want to control your spending, then pay in cash. You are less likely to overspend that way. Plan your daily spending as much as you possibly can. You didn't get into financial trouble overnight and you won't get out overnight. But you do need to make a plan right now.

God has called the men to be the spiritual heads of their homes. I encourage godly men to lead their families in making a plan to get out of debt. If the wife in a marriage is better at bookkeeping or money management, acknowledge the gift; but the man should still take the lead to initiate and develop a financial plan with his wife.

Meet the God Who Teaches You to Profit

Are you tired of bouncing from financial crisis to financial crisis? Are you ready to live the abundant life? Put the Lord first and plan now for financial security and blessings tomorrow.

> I am the Lord your God who teaches you to profit and who leads you in the way you should go (Isa. 48:17).

Ask God to show you how to profit and how to cut expenses. Thousands of Bible verses show us how to properly use and manage money. One of the fruits of the Spirit is self-control. Do you go into a store and just buy anything you want, or do you exercise self-control? Your goal should be to build financial stability for your life and for your family.

Jesus said, "He who is faithful in a very little thing, is faithful also in much. He who is unrighteous in a little thing is unrighteous in much" (Lk. 16:10). If you are faithful with two talents then you'll be faithful with five talents. But if you're not faithful with the one talent, what makes you think that God's going to give you two?

God can only bless you if you properly manage what you have right now. Make up your mind right now to be a *money manager*. The Bible says a good man leaves an inheritance to his children and his children's children. Money spent on clothes and jewelry is wasted money, but money put into your home or property will build generational wealth for the future.

Possess the Land—I Mean It

The best way to accumulate wealth is to be a property owner. God told us to possess the land and He meant it. Since property creates generational wealth, make a strategy to change your spending so you can pass along your blessings to your children.

Rent payments and mortgage payments are about the same, so it is better to own your home. If your credit is a problem, then request a credit report and take an honest look at your credit rating.

The three companies are Experian, TransUnion and Equifax. You can get one free credit report a year, so contact them by phone or by Internet. You will probably find a number of erroneous "bad things" on your credit report, and as you contest them they must be removed.

Pay off the smaller debts on your credit report first, and renegotiate payments on the large ones. Then watch to see how God begins to help you.

People on staff right now recently purchased homes who had never owned property before. Some of them had no money for a down payment, but they moved into a brand new home. Others had some credit problems, but they received enough money back at their closing to pay off the debts that were bad credit on their credit report!

Favor is better than money. If you serve God and obey Him; if you put Him first, the favor of God will come upon you.

Creditors generally look for a 24- month history to evaluate your credit status. If you've had bad credit for a long time, it will take 24 months to set the record straight.

An easy way to reestablish or raise your credit score is to get one low credit limit credit card and charge things on it—then *pay it off in full* each month. Even if you make payments, make sure you *pay on time* every month.

Be honest with your creditors. The worst thing you can do is avoid a creditor. Tell them, "I can't pay the $200, but I can send you $50 this week." Be honest and quit trying to avoid them, and they will work with you.

Do You Believe That God Wants You Blessed?

If you put God first and use your faith, I believe that God will supply you the down payment for a home. If you believe that God wants you to be blessed, then start believing to be a property owner. Confess that in the next few years you are going to own your own property. Even if you have to start with a small condo, at least it's going to be yours.

> *"Become a faithful steward of what you have and make a plan to get out of debt."*

I received a letter from a lady who received this word. She got into an inexpensive condo and began to fix it up. Within a year she sold it for a good profit and bought a bigger condo. She sold that and finally bought her own house.

The Bible says, "Beloved, I pray that in all respects you may prosper and be in good health, just as your soul prospers" (3 Jn. 1:2). It is God's will that you be blessed and relax in your health and in your finances as your soul prospers. As you mature in the Lord, He expects you to become a better money manager and to have more finances at your disposal.

Finance your home over 15 years instead of the usual 30 to build generational wealth rapidly. Your home will be paid off in half the time, the payments will only be about 20% more, but you will get a bigger deduction on your taxes, and you will immediately start building equity (ownership value) into that home.

Financial problems can add a lot of stress to your life. Become a faithful steward of what you have and make a plan to get out of debt. Be faithful over the little things so God can entrust you with bigger things.

The Bible says that the wealth of the wicked is being stored up for the righteous. In other words God will transfer wealth into the hands of true believers in the last days, but only the hands of those He can trust with it. It's time to make a plan to get out of debt.

Financial failure is not the end if you know how to begin again and avoid the mistakes of yesterday. It is time to possess the land, and you win the first battle with the decision to become a good money manager.

In my book, *Keys to Financial Freedom*, I outline how to establish a budget and tap the biblical keys to a good financial life. For more information, visit our Internet website at www.DLministries.com).

Day 16

FROM FAILURE TO FINANCIAL BREAKTHROUGH

Praise the Lord! Blessed is the man who fears the Lord, who delights greatly in His commandments. His descendants will be mighty on earth; the generation of the upright will be blessed. Wealth and riches will be in his house, and his righteousness endures forever. Unto the upright there arises light in the darkness; He is gracious, and full of compassion, and righteous (Ps. 112:1-4).

The Bible tells us wealth and riches are in the house of the man who fears the Lord and delights in His Word. Since I love the Lord, I expect God to bless me in all that I do!

Riches are about having more than enough. You can define riches any way you want, but it is about having *more than enough* emotionally, physically, spiritually, etc.

God wants you to have spiritual, physical, and emotional wealth; but when He speaks of riches, God is really referring to money. So wealth and riches are two separate things.

> "If you will get this message in your spirit today, things will begin to change in your finances."

Everything seems to go better when we have enough money. Our lives, our relationships, our happiness improves when we have enough money.

The goal however is not just to accumulate wealth for wealth's own sake. The goal is to bless others while we are being blessed. The goal is to be a giver because that is the nature of God.

If you take on an attitude of being a giver, God will honor it and He will give back to you. If you take on an attitude of helping others, then God will supernaturally help you. If you bless others, God will bless you.

Christians around the world are struggling with debt, and many are wondering if their failure in finances is the end. No, your whole life will change when you take the focus off of yourself and put the focus on blessing and helping other people! Most of us are paying on car notes, rent/mortgages, credit cards, and doctor's bills; we barely have enough to make it from paycheck to paycheck.

Sometimes people get so far behind that they literally can't see the light at the end of the tunnel. But God has some answers.

He has an anointing that will help you get out of debt! If you will use your faith in the Lord, He will bring a financial breakthrough that will start in your life today.

If you will get this message in your spirit today, things will begin to change in your finances. Psalm 35:27 says that God *delights* in the prosperity of his servants. If I'm serving the Lord today, then God delights in blessing and prospering you and me! It is literally His desire that we walk in financial success.

I'm going to give you seven keys to a financial breakthrough in your life. I firmly believe that if you follow these seven keys and mix your actions with *faith,* then you will see a miracle take place in your life.

Key #1: Make a plan. If you are in debt, then make a plan to cut costs and to become a diligent money manager. Manage *what you have right now* rather than wait for some mythical money ship to come in. Start managing the resources that you have right now. Jesus praised the wise money managers in the "Parable of the Sower," but He was less than impressed with the servant who buried his talent in the ground (see Mt. 25).

God cares about how we manage money and all of the other resources He entrusts to us. Become a wise money manager right now. Cut costs, cut up your credit cards, pack sack lunches for work and school. Do what you have to do to cut those costs and become a good money manager.

Habbakkuk said, "Write the vision, and make it plain upon tables" (Hab. 3:2). Something will happen when you write down the things you believe God will do in your life. It brings a new focus and fresh faith.

What is your vision? What are your specific financial goals? To own your home or business? Write it down and use your faith in the Lord. Add up and summarize your bills and then ask God to help you achieve a breakthrough in your finances.

Jesus encourages persistence! He said we should "ask and *keep on asking*, seek and *keep on seeking*, knock and *keep on knocking*" (Mt. 7:7). Ask the Lord to show you how to manage your money and make wise investments.

Make no mistake, when you use your faith in the Lord, He can cancel debt in an absolute moment! He can move finances instantly. Do not limit God, no matter how outrageous it looks.

God wants you to get a house more than you could possibly imagine. Your spiritual enemy does not want you to get out of debt, but Jesus came to give you the abundant life.

The enemy wants you to be so far in credit card debt that you can't see the forest for the trees. Whatever you are willing to tolerate will stay in your life! Sometimes you have to get sick and tired of being sick and tired of being in debt.

As long as you are in debt, you will never be able to put the Lord first the way you should. When you get out of debt, you can obey God in a whole new way in your life. Debt is bondage, and God does not want you to be in bondage.

Getting out of debt is like building a house. You need a blueprint. Then you need to count the cost. Finally, you put faith and action together. You can get out of debt! Stay focused to accomplish your goals.

Make your plan, plant your seed in good ground, trust in the Lord with all your heart and lean not on to your own understanding. The journey to financial freedom begins the moment you decide that God wants you to be blessed. A journey is a process—you start here, you end up there. Are you ready to be blessed?

Key #2: Stand on the Word. God's Word is mighty and powerful. When you know what God's Word says about your finances, everything will change in your life. If God's Word says you can have it, then you can have it. If it's not in the Word, you can't have it. If you are truly going to be blessed in your finances, then you must *know* what God says about it.

When you know that God delights in the prosperity of His servants; when you know that God wants you to prosper, it is a lot easier to use your faith to get out of debt. When Joshua was going into the Promised Land, God said, "The whole thing is yours, son. Go in and take it. It belongs to you. I said it is yours."

The Promised Land is yours, but you must be strong and courageous to possess it. Once you know what God says about your finances, then you also know He has a breakthrough with your name on it!

Key #3: Always obey the Word. If I will diligently obey God and His Word, He will command His blessings on me. God blesses obedience. The flesh always wants to take shortcuts, but if you will go against the flesh and obey the Word of God, He will command the blessing on you. If God commands me to be blessed, then neither man nor devil can stop me from being blessed. If God be for me...

But the bottom line is that if I obey God's Word, His favor will come upon my life. Favor is better than money because if you have God's favor, then you will have the money you need.

The world says get out of debt by using more credit cards, second mortgages, or even bankruptcy. If you obey God's Word, then everything you touch will be blessed. If you obey the word and go against your flesh you will become spiritually wealthy.

Once you become spiritually wealthy, God can make you financially wealthy. Don't go after riches; go after God. If you obey the Word and do exactly what God tells you to do in your giving, then you are putting yourself in a position for God to bless you.

When you obey the Word, you position yourself for God to cancel your debt. Suddenly the credit clears up, the contract is approved, the check shows up in the mail. Remember, all the silver and all the gold belong to the Lord. If you obey the Word, then be sure to give a tithe of at least 10% of your income unto the Lord. If you obey the Word, you are going to give, and giving causes God to move on your behalf.

When you become a giver, you touch the heart of God. When you touch God's heart, He can do more for you in five minutes than you can do in a lifetime!

Key #4 Speak faith out of your mouth. Our God is a God of faith, and He responds to faith. Faith isn't a feeling on the inside; faith is an action. Learn to speak faith, even when you don't feel faith. "My God is meeting all my needs according to his riches in Christ Jesus. I will not be broke forever. I'm putting God first, and He is commanding a blessing on me. I'm paying my tithes and giving offerings. Now He will open the window of heaven on my life."

The Bible says that faith is the substance of things hoped for and the evidence of things not seen (Heb. 11:1). Faith is right now. I am believing that God is releasing me from my debts *right now*. If you want to see a creative miracle in your health or your finances, then open your mouth and confess what you believe God will do.

Key #5 Be careful what you say. Death and life are in the power of the tongue (Pr. 18:21a). You will eat the fruit of what you are saying. That is why we can't be speaking negative things. Come into agreement with the things of God. Don't cancel your faith by speaking negative.

> *"God's system is about being a giver first."*

And as you plant your seed in good soil, and then water your seed with your prayers, you can expect a harvest to come in. If you don't like the crop you are reaping, change the seed you're sowing. I believe that if you're careful what you say and target your faith, you can see a turn around in your life.

Jesus said, "Give, and it will be given to you; good measure, pressed down, shaken together, running over, they will pour into your lap. For by your standard of measure it will be measured to you in return" (Lk. 6:38).

Step #6 Continually sow seed toward your miracle. Jesus said that if you give, He would touch the hearts of others to give back to you (see Lk. 6:38). God's system is about being a giver *first*. In Gen. 2:8. God had planted a garden toward the East in Eden and there he placed a man whom he had formed. This is my point: *The Lord planted so He could get increase.*

The world tells you to hoard your money but God says to plant your seed if you want to get out of debt. God's system is seed-time and harvest, giving and receiving. You reap whatever you sow! When you plant your seed, you can receive the 30/60/100 fold return.

The tithe rebukes the devourer. However, I believe *the offering brings back the 30/60/100 fold return.* Your job is not enough to take care of you—all it can provide is your "seed corn" for sowing. Quit looking to your job as your sole source of income.

Key #7: Be patient. Through faith and patience you shall obtain the promises of God (see Heb. 6:12). The soil produces a crop by itself—first the blade, then the head. Then the mature grain, and when the crop permits it, he puts in the sickle because the harvest has come.

Plant your seed by faith and don't worry about it. Cover it and water it. It's a process, so quit trying to rush everything. See your giving as planting seed, and your faith will kick in. There is a time to plant, and there is a time to reap a harvest. You plant, water, and in due season you get a breakthrough.

(The beginning of a breakthrough for you is only one decision away. We are dedicated to serving you, so don't hesitate to contact us through our Internet website at www.DLministries.com).

Day 17

CHANGE IMPROVES YOUR LIFE

〰️

We all resist change. It doesn't matter if your skin color is light, dark, or multi-colored. Your background doesn't matter either. We all like the familiar. We like things to be constant in certain areas of our lives.

Some of us may be more adventurous than others when trying new foods, clothing styles, or ministry challenges. Nevertheless, we want *most* of the "furniture" in our lives to always be the same.

We sit in the same seats at church; then we go to the same restaurants after service (and usually order the same favorite entrees). We expect our hair stylists and barbers to do everything just the way we like it. We want to be comfortable.

We say it out loud, we say it in our body language and with our facial expressions at church, at work, and in our living rooms: "Don't make us change. We don't like to change. If it ain't broke, then don't fix it."

Elisha had it made in life. All he had to do to have financial security and status was avoid rocking the boat of what had always been. When the man of God showed up, he saw a glimpse of a new place in God few people know existed, and Elisha decided he had to go there.

This man heard the Word of the Lord, sacrificed his oxen and burned his plow (these were literally part of his inheritance and livelihood), then he turned away from his past and by faith followed God's man into an uncertain future (see 1 Kings 19:19-21).

He left his business and kissed his parents good-bye. Sometimes you have to burn your bridges to the previous way of life and kiss your past good-bye so you can go to a new place in the Lord.

Sometimes you have to get out of the bars and quit hanging around people who drag you down or hold you back. You have to make some changes in your life if you want to go where God wants you to be.

Jesus said, "If anyone wishes to come after Me, let him deny himself, and take up his cross daily, and follow Me" (Lk. 9:23). By definition, the Christian life is a life of change. This is precisely why I say change improves your life.

Why do we do the *same thing* year after year and expect *different results*?

Is God talking to you right now about burning your past and kissing it all good-bye? The rewards are worth every bit of the sacrifice involved.

Put God first and get involved in your church. Give your tithes joyfully and sell out to Him. Don't fight change. If you fight change, then you are fighting progress in your life.

Why do we do the *same thing* year after year and expect *different results*? We keep living in the past and yet expect to have a better future. Release the past and seek God's plan for your future. The Bible says that without a vision the people perish (see Pr. 29:18). You must give up the past if you want a future—especially if you want a vision for where God is taking you.

According to Paul, you have to forget what lies behind so you can reach forward to what lies ahead (see Phil. 3:13). Are you stuck in the past? Kiss the past goodbye, embrace the present, and reach out for your future in Christ.

Change Improves Your Life

Progress always requires change. Understand that you cannot change where you have been, but you *can* change where you are going. *If you had a bad past, then get over it and set your course today for a better tomorrow.*

Jesus gave His life on the cross—not so we could preserve and relive our past, but to give us a fresh start on the future. If you are going through the fire, then allow it to get your attention so you can *change.*

Let God Remove the Things That Need to Be Removed

You have to go through things to experience a breakthrough. Everything you are going through today is preparing you for where God is taking you tomorrow. Let Him remove the things that need to be removed so you can be what you must be in Christ.

Don't be discouraged about your track record up to this point. The Bible says, "And we know that God causes all things [even bad things and failures] to work together for good to those who love God, to those who are called according to His purpose" (Rom. 8:28).

When you go through problem, you may feel as if God has forgotten you. The bottom line is that it is a faith issue. No matter what has come against you, God will somehow turn it around for your good if you trust and obey Him. It is only a matter of time until you get to where you need to go, but first you must make some changes.

No matter who we are, setbacks can take place in our lives. You can be going along just fine, rejoicing that everything is so wonderful. Then the rug of life gets pulled out from underneath you. Take heart. *When Jesus is the Lord of your life,* there is something about change that will improve your life.

From Tragedy to Triumph, From Mess To Message

God tells us to seek His kingdom and His righteousness first, and then He will add in everything we need (see Mt. 6:33). Put Him first, and watch Him take every setback and turn it into a comeback! Jesus Christ is the King of kings and the Lord of lords. Believe that He has the power to turn every tragedy into a triumph and convert every mess into a message. God will transform your failures into successes before it is over.

> "When God is about to move in your life, don't be surprised when the source of your provision dries up."

The Lord uses trouble to take us where He wants us to go. The three Hebrew boys working in the King's palace in Babylon were thrown into a fiery furnace because they took a stand for God, but it became their ticket to promotion (see Daniel 3). Joseph was thrown into an Egyptian prison, but in God's time, his prison term became his ticket to promotion to next in command under Pharaoh (see Gen. 39-41).

After Elijah the prophet prophesied a drought over Israel, God sent him to hide beside the brook Cherith. Everything was wonderful, despite the isolation. The water ran smooth and clean, even in the midst of the drought; and God sent ravens to feed him every morning (see 1 Kings 17).

Then the brook dried up and the ravens disappeared. Elijah could have said, "God, I thought You loved me. Why are You letting me go through this?" Instead, he waited in faith until he heard the Word of the Lord, and then obeyed.

When God is about to move in your life, don't be surprised when the source of your provision dries up. It is as if He says, "Wait a minute. Your destiny is stalled and I must motivate you to change. I'm going to dry up your finances at this sticking point so you will *have* to make a change in your life."

You may not like being in the storm today, but the storm may be carrying the rain of God's blessings because it is forcing you to change. Do you want the power of God in your life—even if it takes a storm to move you into position? Change will improve your life.

Change Improves Your Life

If you want to go to a higher spiritual level, you will have to make some changes. You will have to live by God's standards instead of by how you feel. You must take your values from God's Word instead of the TV network soap opera plots.

God's Fires of Life Have a Way of Forcing Change

If you say you are waiting on God, you might discover that God is actually waiting on you—*to change!* None of us like trouble, most of us only change when we're made to change or when we hurt enough. If we refuse to deal with harmful or sinful issues in our lives, God has a way of turning up the heat. Perhaps you've noticed that the fires of life have a way of forcing change.

Don't fight change, you may find yourself fighting God.

Where there is growth there is change, and where there is change there is growth. Change, alone, doesn't bring growth, but you cannot grow without change.

Are you willing to make changes to find God's will? Will you accept the need for change if it will heal your marriage? Are you willing to get into counseling? Are you willing to praise God in a new way this year?

Whether you know it or not, there are barriers around you. It won't be easy, but you must break through those barriers to change the way God wants you to change.

When my wife and I started the church in our basement, our group grew from just a small handful to about 50 people and we moved to a little storefront. Half of the people left after a power struggle emerged, and God spoke to my heart and said, "Son, get on the offensive."

We had about 50 chairs and only 25 people, but the Lord spoke to my heart and said, "*Order fifty more.* You just lost about half of your little group, but have an offensive thrust and order about fifty more."

Don't Ever Take It Lying Down

I still remember ordering the chairs as if it was yesterday. The Lord showed me a principle that day: *Don't ever take it lying down.*

The Lord showed me a barrier was blocking my way, and it would take an offensive thrust to knock it down! Unless there was a change, I would be in the same place at the same time the following year.

My change began when I obeyed God and purchased 50 chairs we seemingly didn't need. Then God said, "I want you to give like you've never given before." A missionary in India had a great need, and we had $5,000 dollars in the bank. The Lord said, "Give it to him, and then give him another $1,000 dollars a month for 12 months." We obeyed and God blessed.

Push through the barriers in your life. Begin to pray. Make up your mind that you are not going to stay where you are (and accept the fact there has to be change in your life). If you need a break-through in your marriage, your finances, or your ministry; you must be willing to sow seed when you don't want to.

Are you ready to go to a new place in the Lord? Are you willing to step out of your comfort zone? It takes persistence to overcome resistance. What is God telling you to change? Is it a temper problem, prejudice, submission to authority, laziness, unforgiveness, or pride?

Stop playing it safe and launch out into deep water. It is time to get out of the boat of sameness and safety. Step onto the sea of faith and change. It is time to do some water walking by faith. Put your past behind you, embrace the change, and do the new things God lays before you. Even though you have failed in the past, failure is never the end when you put God first.

(We are dedicated to serving you and God's kingdom in any way we can. Don't hesitate to contact us through our Internet website at www.DLministries.com).

Day 18

DON'T GET DOWN ON YOURSELF

> But you are A CHOSEN RACE, A royal PRIEST-HOOD, A HOLY NATION, A PEOPLE FOR God's OWN POSSESSION, that you may proclaim the excellencies of Him who has called you out of darkness into His marvelous light; for you once were NOT A PEOPLE, but now you are THE PEOPLE OF GOD; you had NOT RECEIVED MERCY, but now you have RECEIVED MERCY (1 Pet. 2:9-10).

Look at yourself in the "Mirror of God." God says of man, "as he thinketh in his heart, so is he" (Pr. 23:7). If you *think* you are no good, then you will live that way. That is why you should look at yourself in the "mirror" of God's Word. Don't let society label you—find out what God says about you.

God says we are a royal priesthood, a holy nation, the people of God, His sons and daughters, and joint heirs with Jesus Christ. Are these the titles and rank conferred on you in your home as a child or on the brutal battlefield of the school playground?

Reprogram your mind and heart with the Word of God. It is powerful and sharper than a two-edged sword (see Heb. 4:12). The Word is more powerful than every failure in your life, and all of the "put-downs" and insults you have ever had to endure. God's Word possesses all power to overcome the way you were raised or not raised, but you must get it on the inside your heart.

You may have failed, but that doesn't mean you are a failure. Continue to learn from your failures, but begin again and say, "Things are different now! That low self-worth used to hold me down, but I'm hearing a new sound now. The Word of God is saying better things about me and I believe!"

Some people have been so beaten down by the low comments of other people that they have begun to believe all of the bad news. Again, the solution is God's Word. Remember, "faith cometh by hearing and hearing the Word of God" (Rom. 10:17, KJV).

Your spiritual enemy wants you to get down on yourself and accept the lies that you are ugly, or no good, or nothing but a failure. He desperately wants you to believe that no one could love someone like you. Consider the source! Jesus said, "...he is a liar, and the father of lies" (Jn. 8:44b).

This is important because if you don't think much of yourself, you will have a lousy life, a lousy marriage, and generally lousy relationships. You may be tempted to blame everyone but yourself (and you probably won't like the people around you).

No Clue About How Special They Are...

My wife and I are just amazed at the number of wonderful people we meet who have no clue about how special they are. They pick people as friends and mates that are way beneath them. They will go out with people who aren't near good enough for them because they don't know how unique they are—inside and out. They don't know their true worth because they have been beat down and programmed to think that is all they deserve.

Don't Get Down On Yourself

Because of low-self worth we think we can never own our own home or start our own business. It is time to let God "put your act together" and show you *who you are* in Christ. Put the pain of the past behind you and get reprogrammed with the Word.

Above all, quit listening to the lies of the enemy. Declare the truth in Christ: "I did not evolve from a tadpole or even a monkey. I am created in God's image, and I have given my life to the Lord. Now I have now been adopted into the royal family of God because He loves me."

Don't get down on yourself; get high on God and His love for you. Teach your children to love themselves just as they are—because God does. Tell them, "God made your nose just like that for a reason. You are His delight."

The bottom line is that you are who you are. When you look in the mirror you ought to be able to say, "I like you." We are not supposed to be the same; we were each created to be different and unique. In any given room or sports arena, you would be hard-pressed to find someone who looks like you. Even if you did find a look-alike, there is not another *you* in the world! Nobody can be as good at being you as you can be.

No Competition For Being You

Only you can do what God's called you to do. You will touch people that nobody else can touch. You have no competition for being you. There's no sense in you being jealous of me—you have your own stuff. You work your own stuff.

And even if life has beaten you down and you don't think much of yourself, Jesus came to turn your situation around. He came to let you know that you're a somebody and not a nobody. See, I may feel like a loser, but God said I'm not a loser. He said I'm a joint-heir with Jesus Christ.

Do you know what joint-heir means? That means whatever belongs to Him belongs to me. No matter who tried to beat you down in the past, when you know who you are in Christ, everything just changes suddenly.

All you have to do is get a hold of God's Word and know that God did not create you to live in failure. He did not create you to be a slave to your past. He created you for victory. You don't have to stay stuck in your past.

You don't have to go through this year all the stuff you went through last year. (I will say this: If you are in sin today, you had better get out of it if you want to be an overcomer).

Make up your mind to live for the Lord. Put your shoulders back and know that you're a joint-heir with Jesus Christ, the King of kings and the Lord of lords.

You can get your act together now. You don't have to wait another six months. You don't have to wait until next year. You can get it together now. It's time for you to know that your healing begins today.

You Are Not A Grasshopper; You are Somebody!

You have got a new family today and our big brother's name is Jesus. God is on your side and He wants to help you. You have to know that greater is He that lives in you than He that lives in the world. You have to know that you're a royal priesthood and a holy nation. You are not a grasshopper; you are somebody!

You can overcome every giant, whether they are named rejection, low self-esteem, abuse, addictions, or failure. *God says* you are more than a conqueror through Christ Jesus who loves you (see Rom. 8:37).

When God told Ezekiel to prophesy to the valley of dry bones, he was telling him to speak life to his dead situation. So what's dead in your life? Are you going to obey the Word or just do what you want to do? He was telling him to prophesy good things to his dead situation. Prophesy good things to the bad situations in your life. That is what faith is all about.

Don't tell me you have faith if you can't speak good into your bad situation. Declare, "My greatest days are still ahead!" Say that when things look worse than they have ever been in your life.

God didn't make you to be failure. He created you to walk in victory. Your words are like the rudder of a ship. I'm in right standing when I confess my sins and His blood covers my life.

Don't Get Down On Yourself

The moment you said, "Lord Jesus, be my Lord," He slipped the robe of His righteousness on you, whether you deserved it or not, instantly putting you in right standing with God.

Made a Winner, Not a Loser

Just remember that God made you to be a winner and not a loser. Quit putting yourself down. Stop talking about all the things you can't do and start saying "I can do all things through Christ who strengthens me" (Phil. 4:13).

Change your words because your future is at stake. Whatever you say is going to come back to you. If God be for me, who can be against me? This is my year to get my act together."

> *"Change your words because your future is at stake."*

And now that you love the Lord there is a lion on the inside of you. There's a fighter on the inside of you. There's a champion on the inside of you. There's a survivor on the inside of you.

Quit dwelling on the past and move forward. The truth is that we all need forgiveness and we all must forgive others. Don't remain stuck in the past. Change your words and change your direction. Don't get down on yourself, fly high in God and say:

> "No weapon formed against me shall prosper. If God be for me, who can be against me? I am the righteousness of God through the blood of Jesus Christ, overcoming all the failures of my past (see Isa. 54:17, Rom. 8:31, 2 Cor. 5:21).

(With the enemy always ready to accuse you falsely, you certainly don't need to help him out. Believe what God says about you and live in victory. We are dedicated to serving you. Don't hesitate to contact us through our Internet website at www.DLministries.com).

Day 19

YOU CAN'T TRUST YOUR FEELINGS

For those who are according to the flesh set their minds on the things of the flesh, but those who are according to the Spirit, the things of the Spirit. For the mind set on the flesh is death, but the mind set on the Spirit is life and peace, because the mind set on the flesh is hostile toward God; for it does not subject itself to the law of God, for it is not even able to do so; and those who are in the flesh cannot please God.

... The Spirit Himself bears witness with our spirit that we are children of God, and if children, heirs also, heirs of God and fellow heirs with Christ, if indeed we suffer with Him... (Rom. 8:5-8,16-17a).

Failure *is* the end for people who are led by their emotions. However, *failure is merely another opportunity for God's power to shine* in the lives of those who are "led by the Spirit" as the sons and daughters of God! (See Rom. 8:14.)

We *must* be led by the Spirit of God and not by circumstances, feelings, or emotions. You can't even be led by what your preacher says *unless* it lines up with God's Word.

> ## "We must be led by the Spirit of God and not by circumstances."

Why? *You cannot see your worst enemy.* The Bible says, "For our struggle is not against flesh and blood, but against the rulers, against the powers, against the world forces of this darkness, against the spiritual forces of wickedness in the heavenly places" (Eph. 6:12).

Your enemy is *not* your neighbor, your spouse, or the worship leader who claims you can't sing. Your mortal enemy is a spirit; the one Jesus called the Devil. He only comes for three purposes: to steal, to kill, and to destroy (see Jn. 10:10). He deals in weapons of deceit, temptation, fear, and confusion.

The enemy's favorite tactic is to "load" those weapons with unique information (ammunition) about your personal sins, emotional scars, sore points, grudges, fears, laziness, uncontrolled passions, and the failures of your past. He hopes to convince you that you are following God when you are not.

Now let me shock you: Your strongest enemy may not be the devil! *Your strongest enemy may be your own flesh* (specifically your emotions and feelings).

They Talk the Talk, But Don't Walk the Walk

God wants us to quit acting like carnal Christians. Carnal Christians are worldly Christians who act like sinners. They think they can sleep around, do drugs, lie, and live like they want to. *They talk the talk, but don't walk the walk.*

God expects to see the fruit of the spirit in our lives as we walk in joy, love, peace, patience, and kindness. If your daily life is marked more by depression than by peace, then you are not hooked up with

You Can't Trust Your Feelings

God correctly. Something is not right in your relationship because you are being directed by carnal thoughts, feelings and emotions.

Even if you have been a Christian for years, if you don't know the Word of God, you are probably led more by your feelings than by the Word. Feelings are nice, but you cannot anchor your life on feelings. You anchor your destiny on the unchanging, rock-solid Word of God.

Follow God's Blueprint for Success

Quit floating in the spiritual ozone trying to become some super-spiritual hero. Plant God's Word deep in your heart, allowing it to saturate every thought with the thoughts of God. Stay in the Word because it is your answer and your protection. God's Word is your blueprint for success.

Maturity comes by standing on God's Word regardless of what your emotions may say. Emotions change constantly, but God's Word *never* changes. Maturity says, "Do everything you know to do, and stand upon God's Word, even though your flesh wants to run away!" In contrast, your flesh wants to quit or simply indulge its desires.

Compromise often comes in because we have so many wounds in our lives. Wounds from the past interact with unhealthy emotions to give your spiritual enemy great power to misguide and misdirect you through your feelings. You can't trust your feelings.

We don't like to talk about the weakness we see in ourselves. It is easier to blame somebody else than to admit our own weaknesses and failures. Remember how the enemy uses your feelings against you. Don't let your feelings lock your life on an endless roller coaster ride. Learn what God says, stand on His Word, and refuse to be moved by your circumstances.

Emotional wounds are very much like physical bruises—they don't hurt until you touch them. Wounded emotions look fine to outside observers *until* someone touches those wounds through actions or words.

Very few people reach adulthood without being wounded or scarred through betrayal, disappointment, or rejection. Those wounds may keep you from building healthy relationships in your life.

Some of us realize we need help when deep wounds come, but others may not even realize there is a problem in their heart. They tend to blame everyone else for their unhappiness and they push everyone away. (If you would like someone to help you navigate through some difficult life issues, contact our ministry on the internet at **www.DLministries.com**)

Lord, Heal Everything That Is Broken In My Life

How can Jesus bind up your wounds if you refuse to admit that they exist? Admit you have issues and pray: "God, it is true that I am wounded and hurt. I know I have to forgive some people, so I begin by laying my life on Your altar. I forgive those who hurt me, please heal everything that is broken in my life."

You don't have to grow up in Christ to go to heaven, but it is the only way to receive God's blessings during your stay on the earth! If you live by emotions, then you won't live by God's Word unless you *feel* like it. That means you reap all of the unpleasant consequences that disobedience brings.

Emotion-driven individuals find it nearly impossible to keep their word or to submit to authority. "I know more than they do, and I feel they are wrong. So why should I submit to them?" You'd never say it out loud, but that is the *feeling* behind an attitude of rebellion against authority.

The early history of human flight was a bloody one because it is not safe to fly by your feelings or instincts in the darkness or in storm clouds. Pilots with "Visual Flight Ratings" can only fly in good weather when they can "fly by sight." Only pilots with "Instrument Flight Ratings" can fly when the cloud cover is close to the ground or in difficult weather.

Why? When a pilot flies into a heavy cloud or fog layers, it is very easy to become confused. Even "up" and "down" can be reversed. Pilots have been known to plow right into the side of mountain while flying upside down! They "pulled up" knowing they were coming close to a mountain, but they didn't realize they were actually upside down!

You Can't Trust Your Feelings

"Faith Flight Rated" Pilots Navigate By God's Word

God wants us to "live by faith and not by sight" (see 2 Cor. 5:7). Mature Christians do *not* trust their emotions for navigation through life. They are "Faith Flight Rated" because they have learned to navigate by God's Word, and not by sight or feelings.

Life inevitably takes you into a storm when right appears to feel wrong and wrong appears to feel right (this is especially common where hormones and romantic feelings are concerned).

Don't go by your feelings. Live and walk according to the Word of God, because what you feel may literally cause your destruction.

Navigation is the process of "steering a course" accurately and safely from one place to another. All navigation or direction-finding requires a compass. It takes a compass to pinpoint true North in a storm or a tall stand of trees where no landmarks can be seen. God's Word is our eternal compass for life and eternity, and it towers above all trouble and human failure, totally unaffected by earthly circumstances or interference.

Stop living by your emotions and do what God's Word says. Failure is never the end for Christians who live in obedience to God's plan. If you follow God's blueprint for success, then you will prosper.

> Beloved, I pray that you may prosper in all things and be in health, just as your soul prospers (3 Jn. 1:2, NKJV).

(Feelings can't be trusted, but we can always trust God. Don't hesitate to contact us through our Internet website at www.DLministries.com).

Day 20

THE CONTROL FREAK

But if you are led by the Spirit, you are not under the
Law. Now the deeds of the flesh are evident, which
are: immorality, impurity, sensuality, *idolatry, sorcery,
enmities, strife, jealousy, outbursts of anger, disputes,
dissensions, factions, envying*, drunkenness, carous-
ing, and things like these... (Gal. 5:18-21a).

No matter who we are, *we all have controlling tendencies*. If we
are not careful, these controlling ways will hurt people. We will
hurt their feelings and it will limit our success.

Step up and honestly evaluate and judge yourself *so God won't
have to*. If you frankly examine yourself and make godly changes,
your life will be happier, those around you will be happier, and you
will even have more money come your way. We will enjoy greater
measures of success in life because we will get along well with others better, which affects every single part of our lives.

Pressure seems to bring out our controlling ways, and stress may even flush out the hidden dictator of the soul! If success is measured by how we treat others, then it should be obvious that we need to learn how to give up control.

- Control freaks compulsively push people to get what they want, but most of them don't know they are controlling. If you mention it, most control freaks will have a list of "good reasons" to justify what they do. And nearly every control freak you meet will tell you that *everybody else* is the problem, not them.

- If you are a controller, then I promise you that you are not an easy person to get along with. However, once you recognize your controlling ways, you can make some adjustments and learn how to treat other people better.

- Some of the single people in God's kingdom are unmarried because they are control freaks. Their compulsive controlling pushes people right out of their lives, and they never realize what they are doing.

- A control freak sees a "Do Not Disturb" sign but ignores it and goes in anyway, thinking, *I see it, but this sign would never apply to me.*

- Controllers cannot stand to be told no.

- They have a hard time sitting through any message about praying and waiting on God.

- The last thing a controller wants is to wait on any thing or anyone. They are controllers.

- Control freaks secretly admit they would put God on a schedule if they could!

- Controllers find it difficult to delegate authority. Something inside of them knows they are the only one that knows how to get it done right.

The Control Freak

- When a control freak does delegate authority, he may let somebody else go do it—but then they will have to "go make it better" once the job is complete.

- The actions of control freaks rob others of their confidence and demeans them.

- Control freaks usually have very good ideas, but they are determined to make sure everybody sees their point of view.

- Controllers feel they don't need anyone else's input because they have all the answers. They must win at all costs. They've got to be right. They have to defend themselves, defend their position no matter what it costs.

- If anyone resists their controlling ways, they immediately perceive it as an attack on them. Then they will operate out of anger, or sarcasm, or even a cold shoulder or the silent treatment.

- Anytime the plans of a control freak succeed, they want everybody to know how they succeeded. But when they fail, what they do is say things like, "It's not my fault. They didn't do what I told them to do.

- Control freaks *are the most critical people you will ever meet.*

- *The control freak is not flexible.* The control freak is demanding like a drill sergeant, and they will bark out orders to people around them.

I know of one good way to handle a control freak—when they take over, *just let them do the whole thing.* The problem is that they are so pushy that *they hurt people and they don't know it.*

Controllers are usually very good at their jobs, but they can be condescending and harsh toward others. This is their greatest shortcoming, because success is often determined by how you get along with others.

Part of the problem is that control freaks cannot live with uncertainty. That is why they feel driven to settle any disagreements or problems "right now." To them, control means security, and lack of control means insecurity. They can't pray and wait on God because—again—they have to settle it right now. Why? It is because they are driven by fear.

The Vicious Circle of Fear and Selfishness

People who are driven by fear are usually very defensive. Defensive people don't listen well. Fearful people are always afraid that won't get their needs met so they often become control freaks to protect themselves, so they easily become self-centered. Unfortunately, relationships often fail because of selfishness. It is a vicious circle.

If you were doing something to harm a relationship, wouldn't you want to know about it? If your attitudes were keeping you from prosperity and success, wouldn't you want to know so you could make some corrections in your life?

"Don't let fear guide your life."

Relationships are supposed to be equally fulfilling, so when one person in a relationship is too selfish, needs are not met equally. The truth is that selfish people are hard to get along with.

The Bible says that fear is a doorway into our lives. Make no mistake, when we operate in fear instead of faith, we will always fail as believers. So fear is keeping you from being blessed. God said that if you step out in faith and do what He's told you to do He will meet you at your point of need. Don't let fear guide your life.

For most of my life, I was afraid that something bad was going to happen. I constantly struggled with negative thoughts. Then I discovered that I was a control freak and driven by fear. Control freaks become their own worst enemy.

You Can Destroy That Spirit of Fear

Control freaks are always at odds with somebody. Remember that the root of all control issues is fear. When you make a decision to step out in faith, you can destroy that spirit of fear that's trying to stop you.

The Control Freak

One day I made up my mind that fear was not going to control me. I had finally reached the point in my life where I said, "Wait a minute. I will not let fear cause me to walk in jealousy."

You have to make up your mind that fear is not going to control you.

One day I made up my mind to delegate authority and to give up control. What I'm talking about is we were down in the little storefront church. We used to go in and clean the floors and clean the bathrooms and take care of the sound. We used to do all of that stuff ourselves.

The Lord spoke to my heart one day in the storefront and said, "Son, as long as you have to control everything in this church, your church will stay small. Until you learn to give up control and trust Me and trust people, you will not grow."

Control freaks hold on so tight that they cannot grow in relationships, in their business, in their ministry, or in their finances. The Lord showed me that this was one of my problems in the early days of our church.

God spoke to me about a dozen years ago and He said, "Son, learn to enjoy the journey. What good is it to go through this life and realize when it's all over you that you didn't enjoy your life? You didn't enjoy all the things I had for you."

About ten years ago I began to make some changes in my life. I began to travel and go on vacations. It was time for me to enjoy my life and the things that God had done for me.

Set Boundaries With Controlling People

It's important to learn how to set boundaries with controlling people. When they intrude into your life, you must speak up. You don't have to apologize. Simply set your boundaries in love so they know that they cannot run over you.

The majority of people who fail at work do so because they do not communicate properly, and because of it they don't get along with others as well as they should. Good communication is a key to a successful marriage, to a successful career, and to a successful ministry.

If you do not get along well with people in personal relationships, you will probably be a loner all of your life. We must deal with issues in our lives that would keep us from getting along with others. That even goes for pastors—if you don't get along well with others, you will have limited success.

Emperor Frederick ruled the Holy Roman Empire during the thirteenth century, and he wanted to find the original language of the world. He had the idea that if babies are born and they never hear a particular language, then the "original language" might emerge naturally from them when it came time to speak.

So he took a group of infants from their mothers and had some nurses raise the group. They maintained complete silence when they were with the babies. Tragically, *every single baby died* because of a lack of communication!

Communication is so important that people will die, at least on the inside if they don't have proper communication. Keep the lines of communication open between you and the people around you at home, in the church, and on the job. Otherwise, the enemy may come in and drive a wedge between you.

You Cannot Control a Control Freak

If you have a control freak in your life, make no mistake: *You cannot control a control freak.* In fact, control freaks gain power when you resist them. You can't change them, but you can change yourself.

The law of change says that things don't stay the same. Relationships either get stronger or weaker, but they don't stay the same. Things either get better or worse. But they don't stay the same.

The real issue for control freaks is a lack of trust. Somewhere along the line they got hurt, and they made up their minds that nobody was ever going to hurt them again. They don't trust anybody or anything. They even find it hard to totally trust God or themselves.

For all of these reasons and more, we must get into the Word of God and remove all compromise from our lives. Make the choice right now to walk in faith and not in fear. Take the mask off and leave it at the cross—you won't need it.

Let go of any need to control and learn to put God in control of your life. Put your trust and faith in Him, for He is faithful. Finally, walk by faith and not by sight.

(It isn't easy to overcome a compulsion to control everything, but it is worth the fight. Don't hesitate to contact us for help or prayer by visiting our Internet website at www.DLministries.com).

Day 21

THE CRISIS OF FAILURE IS A TURNING POINT

And on that day, when evening had come, He said to them, "Let us go over to the other side." And leaving the multitude, they took Him along with them, just as He was, in the boat; and other boats were with Him. And there arose a fierce gale of wind, and the waves were breaking over the boat so much that the boat was already filling up. And He Himself was in the stern, asleep on the cushion; and they awoke Him and said to Him, "Teacher, do You not care that we are perishing?" And being aroused, He rebuked the wind and said to the sea, "Hush, be still." And the wind died down and it became perfectly calm. And He said to them, "Why are you so timid? How is it that you have no faith?" (Mark 4:35-40).

No matter who you are, the time will come in your life when a storm will fill the horizon, darken your view, and push you to the brink of decision or change. We call this a crisis, and we will *all* face a crisis of some kind in our lives.

Crises come and go, welcomed or not. The real question is, "How will you weather the crisis when it comes?"

> "Be realistic about life."

The original Greek root word for crisis means simply "decision." The first dictionary definition I found for *crisis* was "a turning point for better or for worse in an acute disease or fever." It is also "an unstable or crucial time or state of affairs in which a decisive change is impending...a situation that has reached a critical stage."[1]

Every crisis you face will become a turning point for better or for worse. We have a *better outlook* for those who have laid their lives before the cross of the Lord Jesus Christ. This is our promise:

> And we know that *God causes all things* [good and bad] to *work together for good* to those who love God, to those who are called according to His purpose (Rom. 8:28).

As we look at this story you can see the disciples, along with Jesus, were going across the lake. A storm arose and the disciples definitely faced a crisis!

Be realistic about life. If Abraham, Moses, Elijah, Isaiah, John the Baptist, Jesus Christ, the disciples, and Paul *all faced crises in their lives*, why would you somehow be exempt?

Take Courage, I Have Overcome!

Times of crisis and failure *will come*. The Bible says, "Many are the afflictions of the righteous; but the Lord delivers him out of them all" (Ps. 34:19). Jesus said, "These things I have spoken to you, that in Me you may have peace. In the world you have tribulation, but take courage; I have overcome the world" (Jn. 16:33).

If you belong to the Lord and failure or crisis comes, just know that the Lord is going to get you through it.

The Crisis of Failure Is a Turning Point

There is something about a storm that causes *real* believers to dig down deep with their faith. We learn more about the Lord in a crisis than we knew before we faced the crisis.

Faith only grows in human hearts in times of trouble, trial, and crisis. You see, storms have a way of showing us how big God really is! Faith grows each time you face a crisis, begin to trust in the Lord, and then watch Him move on your behalf. (The biggest mistake the enemy can make is send a crisis our way!)

Always remember that your fight is *not with people* or even the storm itself. Your fight is mostly the struggle to hold on to your faith through it all. Do you want a simple test to gauge the strength of your faith? Do you keep on bringing Him your tithes and offerings even when you are facing a crisis? That really shows God that you are fighting for your faith.

Do you have enough faith in Him to prepare for the ministry even when you don't have a place to preach? It is all about hanging on to your faith.

I May Not Have Money, But I Have Some Faith

The Lord wants us to have so much faith in Him that we prepare to own our own business when we don't have any money. You see it's a faith issue. It's about trusting in Him. He wants us to have so much faith in Him that we drive around on Sunday afternoon looking at houses even though we don't have the down payment. "I may not have the money yet, but I've got some faith."

The Lord wants us to have so much faith in Him that we start preparing for a husband or wife, even though we haven't had a date in five years. We've got to get into counseling before God brings us that man or that woman. We've got to be in premarital classes before He brings that man or that woman.

If you are in a storm today, don't let it get you down. This crisis is all part of God's plan to strengthen and cleanse you. It is the only way God can teach you how to walk by faith and not by sight. A crisis will teach you how to trust in Him and to never, ever quit.

Don't panic because you are in a crisis. A crisis is simply a turning point in the Kingdom of God. If you are facing trouble, remember God's

147

Word and trust Him to make your crisis work to your good. It is just a turning point.

The storm of crisis is all about increasing your faith. When you have real faith, you will go through the storm and not get angry at God. You will keep coming to church, even though you have been disappointed.

Refuse to Let Trouble Steal Your Peace

When you have real faith, you keep on tithing when your mind says you that you can't afford it, just so you can rub it in the enemy's face. If you have real faith, you refuse to let trouble steal your peace—even when you have to go against your emotions and feelings to obey the Word of God.

Christians who endure crisis with real faith obey God even when things don't look as if they are working out in their lives. They forgive people who don't deserve to be forgiven, simply because Jesus commands it.

Crisis produces and reveals real faith that is persistent. This is *not* the "hot-house tomato" variety of faith that can only flourish in good times, controlled climates, and perfect scenarios. It isn't "classroom faith" favored by academics who rarely venture out of ivory towers into the crisis-filled reality of real life.

Real faith; the woman with the issue of blood had it.

This woman faced a life and death crisis. She was at the end of her options; her doctors bled her dry of money and in the end gave her no hope. By their confession, this woman was destined for an early appointment with the grave.

She kept saying in her heart and with her mouth, "If I can touch Him, I shall get well. If I can press through the obstacles, I shall get well."

Death and life are in the power of the tongue. This woman was saying, "I shall get well." Today we can look back to what Jesus has already done and say, "By His stripes I am already healed!" It's not easy to say this when you are not feeling too good.

The Crisis of Failure Is a Turning Point

She Pushed Her Way Through the Doubt and Unbelief

This woman pressed through every discouragement until she touched Jesus. She walked, crawled, and pushed her way through all of the doubt and unbelief and fleshly clamoring until she could touch the Master.

Driven by the urgency of her crisis, this woman persevered through real faith until she was healed by the virtue of God's Son. That is what real faith is all about.

This woman was in a crisis, but she kept fighting for her healing and she was determined to never quit.

Failure quickly separates the immature from the mature, the pathetic from the passionate; the false from the true. Crisis separates the phonies from the faithful. The crisis of failure lets us know what we really believe in and why.

Some years ago, the enemy came in to my life to steal everything I had. But I pursued the enemy. I kept a hold of my faith. I kept on trusting God. And just like Job, God is giving me double for my trouble. He'll do the same thing for you.

So if the enemy comes into your life and brings a crisis, make up your mind to keep on trusting in the Lord. Make up your mind to keep holding on to your faith. Remember that the crisis is just a turning point and the devil can't have your peace.

I remember when I first got saved. Storms would come into my life and the storms would shake my faith. I'd pray for one thing and the opposite would take place.

At first, those setbacks shook my faith. Then I learned that it was the storms that brought the rain of God's blessings into my life.

Believe God and Let the Storm Make You Stronger

God is bigger than any storm threatening to sink you. He is greater than any crisis you face today. Never give up because of a passing storm. Believe God and let the storm make you stronger through the wind and the waves of adversity.

A Roman centurion named Julius and a squad of Roman soldiers were transporting the Apostle Paul to Rome by ship when a violent storm suddenly changed their destinies. The ship's captain and the

Centurion had ignored Paul's warning and sailed into winter seas and harm's way.

When the violent storm began to tear apart the ship, Paul encouraged the passengers and crew and said no lives would be lost because an angel had appeared to him and told him what would come to pass.

Make no mistake: The enemy of God sent that lethal storm hoping to steal Paul's faith, take his life, and possibly destroy the plan of God to plant the gospel in Caesar's household. The ship was totally destroyed, but the words of Paul came true when all 276 people aboard made it safely to the shore of an island that is still called Malta.

After local residents made a fire to welcome the survivors, Paul gathered a bundle of sticks to help stoke the flames. When he leaned over to put the bundle on the fire, a deadly snake "came out of the heat" and fastened itself on Paul's hand.

When the locals saw the poisonous snake hanging from Paul's hand, they were horrified. The sight convinced them Paul was a murderer who deserved to die despite his close call with the shipwreck.

Paul Just Shook Off the Snake

The Bible says that Paul just shook off the snake, dropping it right back into the fire, and went about his business. The locals (and probably the enemy himself) knew what *should* have happened, and what they were sure *would happen*: Paul would either swell up or immediately fall down dead.

Time went by and Paul just kept going until everyone there realized something supernatural had happened—although the apostle treated it as something perfectly natural (see Acts 26 and 27).

Paul didn't let the crisis stop him. He just shook off the enemy's hindrance into the fire. Evidently, the snake didn't know that Paul had already been trained.

This thing had bitten the hand of a man who had already survived five near-death beatings with whips, three beatings with rods and clubs when he was left for dead; had been stoned with rocks, persecuted in every city, and suffered thirst and starvation—how could this man of faith let some little half-baked snake stop him now?

The Crisis of Failure Is a Turning Point

Paul had been shipwrecked three different times. He had faced dangers from criminals and thieves, and from religious folks trying to kill him every time he went into a city. He had government officials hunting him down to destroy him, and had gone without food and water for weeks at a time.

After all that Paul had gone through, there was no way that this little snake crisis was going to stop him. We need to get to the point that we can shake off everything that tries to stop us, knowing all along that it is just a turning point in our lives!

When you've gone through enough, and the storms come their way, you'll sit back and laugh at the enemy and say, "Surely you don't think this is going to take me out."

When you've gone through enough, you'll look at the trouble in your life and say with Paul, "Hey devil, you can't take me out now. My faith in the Lord is too strong." When you have real faith, things that try to get a hold of you won't be able to stick to you.

> *"You may feel as if you are hanging on a cross of your own, but it is just a turning point."*

I May Be Bitten, But I Cannot Be Beaten!

With real faith, you just shake off the things that try to slow you down. Real faith says, "Greater is He that lives in me... I may be bitten, but I cannot be beaten."

Even if the storms of life sink your ship, make up your mind to swim ashore and catch another ship. "You may not want me baby, but somebody does. I'm going to swim ashore and catch me another ship." Remember, the crisis is just a turning point.

It was Friday and it didn't look too good for Jesus hanging on a cross. The devil was winning, or so he thought. But on the third day, Jesus rose from the dead.

You may feel as if you are hanging on a cross of your own, but it is just a turning point. God will turn it all around for good, no matter what. Quit crying over your past. It's time to quit your crying, because somebody doesn't like where you go to church or the color of your skin. Just shake it off and don't let anything steal your faith.

Crises and failures come against all of us, but the Word of the Lord right now is: *When the failures come, don't let anything steal your faith in the Lord*. Every crisis is a turning point. The dictionary says it is for better or for worse—but we operate under different rules than the rest of the world. Pray this prayer with me right now over your failure:

> I'm submitted to God and His Word. I go by what He says, not what people may say. And God is going to turn it for my good. For every crisis in the life of a believer is made to work for good, because You, my God, will carry me through.

> *(God has a way of turning a crisis into a victory. Don't hesitate to contact us if we can help you in any way. Visit our Internet website at www.DLministries.com)*.

Endnotes

1. *Merriam Webster's Collegiate Dictionary, Tenth Edition* (Springfield, MA: Merriam-Webster, Incorporated, 1994), p. 275, "crisis." The first definition was derived from the original etymology or root words in Greek and French. The other definitions noted are direct quotes.

Day 22

TRUSTING GOD DURING THE CRISIS

Beloved do not be surprised at the fiery ordeal among you which comes upon you for your testing. As though some strange thing were happening to you. But to the degree you share the sufferings with Christ, keep on rejoicing so that also, at the revelation of His glory you may rejoice with exaltation (1 Pet. 4:12-13).

You understand that the crisis of failure may really be a turning point in your life, but do you know how to trust God in the *middle* of that failure?

Don't groan and skip over this chapter—it *does* apply to you if you call yourself a believer in Jesus Christ. God has made an appointment for you on His potter's wheel, and He is about to spin that wheel... (see Isa. 64:8, Jer. 18).

The potter's wheel is a stone wheel that looks like a small round tabletop. The master potter takes a lump of clay and plops it in the middle of the wheel and begins to spin it around. Then he wets his fingers and begins to mold and shape the clay.

First he pushes a hole in the center with his fist or fingers, and then raises and forms the sides between his moistened fingers. He may punch down the clay in a ball over and over again, removing unwanted debris or hardened clay lumps before reshaping the clay yet again (and again). The process stops only when the clay has become what he wants it to be.

When you give your life to the Lord, our God puts you on His potter's wheel where He begins to mold you. You love the Lord and you are on your way to heaven, but God has a job for you to do. It is time to speed up that spinning and changing process. After the initial forming and shaping comes the *heat.*

Heat is used to fundamentally change the properties and characteristics of a whole variety of raw materials such as metal, pottery and other clay products (*and* human lives).

When extreme heat is applied to precious metals—or virtually any metal—it converts them to a liquid form and caused the dross— the waste materials and contaminants—to float to the top where they may be skimmed off.

Is God Heating Your Mixture For a Divine Purpose?

Glass is made under high heat as well. You mix sand with lime and soda over a fire that is so hot that these dissimilar materials literally melt together and become a liquid (this is what God does with church families). This is my point: you heat the mixture until it becomes what it needs to be. Is God heating your mixture for a divine purpose?

Sometimes a low fire just won't get the job done. If you overhear someone talking about you behind your back *but it isn't enough to get you to change,* then God may turn up the heat. The refining process must be hot enough to melt away every hindrance or distraction in your life.

Glass and most metals share a common trait—they can both be reheated and converted to a liquid or some pliable form, even after they have been broken. Broken and discarded glass can be reheated, re-melted and reformed just as if it were the first time. You may be broken today, but one pass through the fires of God can reshape you and make you into something custom formed and crafted for the Master's use.

When lower heat values are applied to metals, fine pottery, and clay products such as bricks or tiles; the elements are *tempered* or made strong and resistant to bending, molding, or infiltration by the outside environment.

God often allows us to go through a firing process for specific purposes. In fact, just before He promotes you, He may allow you to go through a fire heated seven times hotter than normal. Just ask Daniel's three young Hebrew disciples about the fire. Before they were promoted in the kingdom of Babylon, they were all thrown into the fiery furnace because they took a stand for God in the face of certain death (see Dan. 3).

> *"God is going to meet you in the fire, so don't worry about it."*

The process hasn't changed. Before God does a work in you, He allows the fires to burn away the contamination and mixture in your life. The fires of heaven will burn up everything that is not of God.

You Have An Appointment With the Fire

Some preachers tell you that if you have enough faith, you won't have any trouble. I don't think so. It is my job to tell you that *you have an appointment with the fire.* God is going to meet you in the fire, so don't worry about it. He will take you through it.

I don't know what you're going through today, but you should pray the way Jesus prayed: "Give us this day our daily bread." Don't worry about tomorrow's bread, just trust God to supply what you need right now. "Lord, give me what I need today. I'm not worried about tomorrow. Tomorrow is going to take care of itself."

Everything you are going through today *is preparing you for your future.* I know it doesn't feel good sometimes. It feels like you're going to be burned alive, but I have to tell you the truth: *Your miracle is in the fire!* You can't quit now.

If you are going through a fiery ordeal, the apostle Peter said you shouldn't act surprised about it. It comes to all of us. God is going to get glory out of it and you're going to be a changed person when it is all over.

You know the potter's wheel is working when you perceive and believe that God has allowed you to go through the fire *for a reason.* It is working once you quit blaming God and you know in your heart that everything is going to be all right.

Fire Veterans Never Let the Enemy See Them Sweat

You can spot the people who been through the fire of God. They praise God all the time, even in the middle of "hell and high water." Fire veterans never let the enemy see them sweat because *they know that they know* God is faithful.

David said, "It was good for me that I was afflicted." You know that the fire has done its job when you can say, "It was good for me to go through the trouble I endured." If you can't say that about a period in your life, then you do not understand the fires of God.

When the fire is burning, it's a sure sign that God is on the move. It's a sign that your miracle is on the way and God is about to do something in your life. Get ready; something is about to be born in your life.

The fire often begins to burn when you begin to pray, "Lord, change me." The heat begins to rise the day you can say from the heart, "Lord, make me into Your image."

You can't be saved for very long without saying it. "God, make me what You want me to be." At first you may not say it, but after you've been saved for a while, *something inside you says, "Lord, my life is Yours. Conform me to Your image."*

Something inside you will begin to cry out, "I want to be like You. God use me for Your glory." You may not even know what it means, but the process will begin. *That is when the fire begins to burn.*

Trusting God During the Crisis

People who have always been with you suddenly turn against you. The friends you thought would never leave you walk out on you. Folk who were on your side yesterday may change their minds about you today. You didn't change a thing; you didn't do anything differently. You are still the same person, but the fire has begun to burn.

The Only Constants In Life Are God and Change

After all, you *did* pray, "Lord change me." This is the humbling process, the molding time, the breaking season when the only constants in life are God and the certainty of *change*.

If you feel like Shadrach, Meshach or Abed-Nego, and you feel the searing heat from a fire seven times hotter than any you have ever seen, rejoice! *Your miracle is in the fire.* Don't run away, wriggle out, or grab a fire extinguisher. You are about to undergo a change, a transformation so unique that God Himself will join you for communion in the midst of the flames. If you trust in the Lord, you won't even have the smell of smoke on your clothes.

The deeper the builder drills into bedrock, the higher the building is going to be. The more they go into the ground, the higher they plan on building the building. The deeper they go down, the higher they go up. Don't let the crisis steal your faith. If you're going through a lot, remember that the farther He takes you down for a foundation, the higher the Builder will take you in the end.

Don't get upset with God because things are falling apart. Don't quit; God has it all under control. It is a Holy Ghost set-up. You are going through some challenges because He wants your roots to go deep—far deeper than you ever wanted or dreamed. If your roots stay shallow, then any kind of a storm can uproot you.

What If God Wants To Make You Into a Skyscraper?

Some folk are content to live in a little shack next to the railroad tracks, but what if God wants to make you into a skyscraper? He always builds from the foundation up. God is sending your roots down deep because He intends to raise you to a higher place.

To use another analogy, before God takes anyone to a higher level, He allows the fires to burn the things out of you that shouldn't be there.

God chose Moses to lead the children of Israel out of Egypt, but Moses still had too much of Egypt inside of him! God led him into the wilderness to burn the Egypt out of him. Moses was anointed by God but he wasn't ready to lead yet.

You may be anointed to preach, but you are not quite ready to lead yet. Yes, you can sing with the anointing, but He can't quite trust you yet. Get ready. He is about to put you on the Potter's Wheel to remove the spirit of the world out of you. He knows what you need to release, and He also knows how to help you release it.

When you're all by yourself, *you begin to pray in a whole new way.* In fact, had you not gone through that lonely time in your life, you might not be in church today! It is in the lonely times that you learn to trust in God instead of man. That is when God begins to talk to you—and when you finally begin to listen.

If you are all alone, realize it is a set-up. Quit being so needy and desperate. Get your eyes off of yourself and your situation, and put them back on the Lord. Seek Him first.

God Has a Storm That Will Absolutely Rock Your Boat

God loves you too much to leave you in your mess. He corrects and chastises the children He loves. If you go in a wrong direction, He knows how to get your attention. He has a fire that will burn, and a storm that will absolutely rock your boat.

We think we know what's best for us, but most of the time we don't have a clue about God's infinite plans for us. That is why we have to put it in His hands and trust Him for the rest.

Trust the Lord in the middle of the storm and prepare for transformation.

(Transformation can be difficult, even in the best of times. Don't hesitate to contact us if we can help or pray. Visit our Internet website at www.DLministries.com).

Day 23

PRAYER CHANGES SITUATIONS

So Peter was kept in the prison, *but prayer for him was being made fervently by the church to God.* And on the very night when Herod was about to bring him forward, Peter was sleeping between two soldiers, bound with two chains; and guards in front of the door were watching over the prison. And behold, *an angel of the Lord suddenly appeared*, and a light shone in the cell; and he struck Peter's side and roused him, saying, "Get up quickly." And *his chains fell off his hands* (Acts 12:5-7).

There is nothing the adversary dreads more than a praying Christian. The enemy laughs at our programs, snickers at our human abilities, and mocks our wisdom. Yet, he trembles when we pray. Why? It is because prayer will move heaven on our behalf.

The Bible says, "The effective prayer of a righteous man can accomplish much" (Jas. 5:16b). Prayer takes things out of our hands and puts them in God's hands. It is time to quit worrying and start praying.

All kinds of worries and pressures come against your mind, your family, your business, and your finances. Quit worrying about everything. Worry over nothing, pray over everything, and put all things in God's hands.

> *"Worry over nothing, pray over everything, and put all things in God's hands."*

Prayer changes situations. Sadly, the church just doesn't pray enough. More impossible situations would be changed and turned around if we rediscover the power of prayer in Jesus' name.

And whatever you ask in My name, that will I do, that the Father may be glorified in the Son. If you ask Me anything in My name, I will do it (Jn. 14:13-14).

Prayer in Jesus' name opens doors that nothing else can. God only moves in *response* to our prayers. Since Jesus Christ has already defeated the enemy; it must be our lack of prayer that defeats us as Christians. None of us should have to lose sleep due to worry or anxiety because when we belong to the Lord, the victory is already won!

Old Testament Corporate Prayer Was An Ordeal

In the Old Testament, when difficulty confronted Moses and the children of Israel in the wilderness, they faced a major ordeal just to seek God's help as a nation.

All 12 tribes had to stop, make camp, gather and stack stones to form an altar, lay wood on top, and offer a sacrifice. Everyone waited while Moses or the priests offered prayers to God on behalf of everyone else.

We don't have to build altars of stone or ask priests to intervene on our behalf today. You can build an invisible altar of prayer in your car as you drive down the highway, or in your kitchen, office, or on the beach.

Count on it: If you are not praying He is not moving. If you are not praying, the only one moving is your enemy as he infiltrates, contaminates, and decimates your business, your family, your finances, and your destiny. Prayerless people are powerless people.

Modern American churches often have fabulous buildings, choirs, worship bands, state-of-the-art sound and lighting, and television equipment. Without prayer, none of it will succeed. The kingdom of man advances on fleshly deeds, but the Kingdom of God advances on its knees.

Prayer changes situations, but *without* prayer you will be destined for failure! Victory and peace will elude us unless we get back to praying. Only praying Christians will see the enemy defeated in their lives.

Our answers will not come from connections at the White House, they will come on our knees in God's house. Whether you like it or not, you have a spiritual enemy who is totally against you. The reason you must pray is because you need the Lord on your side. We all need His help, strength, direction, and wisdom.

Social Clubs or Prayer Training Centers?

God declared, "For My house will be called a house of prayer for all the people" (see Isa. 56:7b, Mt. 21:13, Mk. 11:17, Lk. 19:46). It seems that many churches today have become social clubs rather than training centers for prayer warriors. We desperately need to get back to prayer in this new millennium. If there was *ever* a day that we needed to know how to pray, it is today! Times are growing worse and worse.

Be diligent in prayer as you cover your children, your family, and your very life in prayer. Jesus modeled diligent, fervent prayer before His disciples and they wanted what they saw in His life. They had watched Him spend entire nights in prayer before spending the following day casting out demons, confronting hypocrites, and healing the sick.

The disciples knew the secret to His power was prayer. Oh, if we could only tap into that secret in our lives! We would walk in the same power Jesus demonstrated on the earth!

Prayer determines the power that you walk in. If there is no power, there is a good chance there is no prayer. So how do you turn things around?

Jesus said, "Ask and keep on asking. Seek and keep on seeking. Knock and keep on knocking" (Lk. 11:9, from the Charles B. Williams translation[1]). In other words, Jesus doesn't want us to pray for one minute and then give up. God is not offended by persistence; He is blessed and moved by it.

I read somewhere that the average Christian prays an average of two minutes per day. God wants us to an attitude of *continual* prayer. As long as prayers go up, the enemy and all of his schemes keep going down. We can't afford to quit praying.

Everything Is Subject to Change When People Pray

We are the family of God and we *must* pray for each other! I challenge you to live a life of prayer because everything is subject to change when people pray in Jesus' Name. Your family needs your prayers. Your boss needs your prayers. Your pastor needs your prayers, so pray!

Jesus said, "Again I say to you, that if two of you agree on earth about anything that they may ask, it shall be done for them by My Father who is in heaven" (Mt. 18:19). Some prayers produce breakthroughs only when they are offered with the power-boost of *agreement* in your life. One can put a thousand to flight, two put ten thousand to flight.

Will you pray and stand in the gap for your neighbor? Remember: God moves primarily in response to the prayers of His people.

True prayer is not about fancy words and ceremonies, prayer beads, prayer manuals, or prayer shawls. It is about prayer and a relationship with the Lord, trusting Him everyday.

Whether you know it or not, *true prayer is hard work*. I used to go into prayer armed with all kinds of prayer lists. Later, I got rid of my lists because it felt as if it was too legalistic. Then I realized that when I stopped using my lists, I stopped praying too.

The point of my story is this: Do whatever works for you. In my case, I found that as long as I had a list to "pray through," it kept me praying persistently and fervently. It caused things to come back to my remembrance. Do whatever it takes to keep yourself on your knees. Prayer changes situations.

It Will Cost You Sleep and Personal Time

True prayer is costly. If you give yourself to the true spirit of prayer, it will cause you to get up in the middle of the night and pray until the need passes. *True prayer is expensive.* It will cost you sleep and personal time, but it yields eternal dividends.

True prayer is about talking and listening, it is about spiritual warfare and supernatural peace, it involves crying and laughing; it is true communion with the Lord.

The first church of Jesus Christ knew how to pray. They walked in the power of the Holy Ghost, healed the sick, cast out demons, saw the lame walk and the blind see. They knew how to pray until prison doors opened and the power of God shook the foundations. They knew how to pray until the heavens opened and God led them out.

If there is a lack of spiritual prayer in your life, then do what it takes to get back to prayer now. Prayer changes things. When you pray, you are placing everything in God's hands. Revivals don't happen unless somebody is praying. Healings don't happen unless somebody is praying. Miracles don't happen unless somebody pays the price in prayer.

As long as you have breath to pray, failure is not the end. Prayer changes things, and fervent prayer shakes things. Fervent and unified prayer in one mind and one accord literally shakes cities, regions, and nations. It is time to get back to prayer.

(Prayer is powerful and it will carry you through virtually every situation. If you do find that you need encouragement or agreement in prayer, don't hesitate to contact us through our Internet website at www.DLministries.com).

Endnotes

1. *The New Testament From 26 Translations* (Grand Rapids, MI: Zondervan Publishing House, 1967), p. 266. Citing Charles B. Williams, "The New Testament: A Translation in the Language of the People.

Day 24

GET THE JUNK OUT OF YOUR TRUNK

Therefore, since we have so great a cloud of witnesses surrounding us, let us also lay aside every encumbrance [weight or hindrance], and the sin which so easily entangles us, and let us run with endurance the race that is set before us (Heb. 12:1).

Imagine stepping onto a running track with 12 lanes and 12 sets of starting blocks. You notice the other runners stretching and making a last minute check on the blocks in anticipation of the upcoming race.

When the home crowd sees you step onto the track, a roar of applause fills the air. You feel the snug fit of your favorite shoes and your legs feel good. There is only one problem...a nagging pain in the right shoulder. With a shrug, you think to yourself, *Someday I'm going to ask the coach about this backpack thing. It sure makes it tough to compete with this thing. It just keeps getting heavier week after week....*

We enter this world naked, unashamed, and burdened only with our helplessness and our family bloodline from Adam. Unfortunately, many of us do not grow up in decent homes where nurture, love, and good examples help shape a normal life in our minds.

Yet, every year from our birth, *all of us* suffer little wounds, hurts, injustices, or even outright abuse. Sometimes it comes from parents unaware of the damage inflicted by their words or anger; very often it comes from painful encounters with brothers, sisters, friends and battles with our peers.

Each incident goes into the invisible "backpack" we carry in our memories and spirit. If these little packets of emotional and spiritual baggage are never cleaned out and put in order, they begin to dominate and entangle our lives.

Everybody, in some way, is dragging and pulling baggage from their past. We carry our backpacks of painful baggage everywhere we go—into our new school, into our new marriage, into our ministry, and sometimes all the way to the grave.

We pull this weight around in our lives, but for some the baggage becomes unbearable to carry any longer and their lives end prematurely in suicide or due to stress-related disease.

Wounded and Insecure People Are Especially Vulnerable

Rejection is the dominant weight in our baggage, and fear is another. Virtually every emotional wound we carry stems from a lack of love. Unfortunately, the enemy knows that wounded and insecure people are especially vulnerable to sin and the infliction of even more pain.

As we grow up in Christ, *we must learn to deal with our hidden baggage*. Don't make the mistake of assuming you have no baggage. You do.

Jesus demonstrated the right way to deal with baggage in his encounter with a man who had a withered hand in a Jewish synagogue. The need was there, and the Healer was there, but the two had to connect.

According to the Bible, Jesus confronted some religious hypocrites who were using the handicapped man as bait to trap Him.

Then Jesus told the man in front of everyone: "'Stretch out your hand!' And he stretched it out, and it was restored to normal, like the other" (Mt. 12:13).

This man had to acknowledge his need and then reach out to Jesus. Only then was God's healing virtue released to heal and restore. First you must say, "God, I need healing in this part of my life." Then God will heal you.

As the years go by we tend to build walls around ourselves. And of course we always want to blame our baggage on somebody else or simply hide it away out of sight. Rather than go to God to find out who we are in Christ, we tend to let our low self-esteem direct us and control us. That is when we take out our baggage to build walls with our packaged hurts and wounds.

Workaholics follow their extreme work ethic seeking more than the esteem they receive from a job well done. They seek to find something that is missing from their lives.

> *"God wants you to slip off that backpack filled with baggage."*

We Lie to Guard Our Pride and Cover Our Baggage

All of us tend then to build protective walls around our weak areas to keep people out. We lie to guard our pride and cover our baggage. We don't want the real truth to get out about who we are. We should go to God and say, "Father, I have a serious pride problem."

The higher we build the walls around our hurts and weaknesses, the more we want to blame others for our problems. We just keep pulling out our luggage and stacking the walls higher.

Again, God's Word says we should do *just the opposite*: "Lay aside every encumbrance [weight or hindrance], and the sin which so easily entangles us, and let us run with endurance the race that is set before us" (Heb. 12:1b).

God wants you to slip off that backpack filled with baggage. Get the straps away from your feet so you won't get tangled up in them any longer. Lay aside the thing that's keeping you from being what God's called you to be. You have a race to run!

Unforgiveness is one of the most destructive forms of emotional baggage that you will ever experience in your life. In theory, we drag around a back-breaking load of unforgiveness on the excuse, "Well, *they* haven't been fair to us!" Life is never going to be fair, but God is a just god. He is keeping track and He is keeping score. Let it go so He can help you.

God Wants to Roll Away All the Things That Hurt You

Now that you are born again, God wants to roll away all the things that hurt you. He wants to roll away the reproach of your past. You are no longer a victim; He has made you more than a conqueror.

If it doesn't happen, your baggage may become so great that even the people who love you may not be able to handle you. You know there is a problem if you swore you would never be like your mother, but now you are driving your husband away just as she drove three of her husbands away.

God is more concerned with healing you than helping you get that new car. He's more concerned about the way you treat others than He is about you getting that new suit. He's more concerned about the baggage you keep dragging around year after year after year, than He is about helping you get a new dress.

Don't expect your friends to help you through all of this. If you have followed the common pattern (and I hope you haven't), then you have attracted people to you who share your problem.

Have you attracted people who have the same junk in their trunk that you have in yours? You must know who God says you are *in Christ*; don't go by what other people say about you.

It Is the Junk In Your Trunk...

That baggage you drag around is the same as junk in your trunk. The reason you can't stand for a man to tell you what to do is because of the junk in your trunk. You can't stand for a woman to boss you because of the junk in your trunk. Do you know why you hate educated people so much? It is the junk in your trunk....

Get the Junk Out of Your Trunk

Most of our trunks have some junk boldly labeled "PRIDE." That is the volatile baggage that makes you lose control, it is the hot button of your behavior. "He's not going to talk to me like that!" "Who does she think she is?!"

Just a brief "stroll" through your emotional luggage room will tell you a lot about yourself. God says *get the junk out of your trunk!*

If you don't deal with it, then what you end up doing is living in a cycle of failure year after year. If you really want to get the junk out of your trunk just ask the people around you what you need to change.

You know you're not emotionally healthy when you blame everybody else for your trouble. You know your trunk is full of junk when you cannot take responsibility for things that go on in your own life.

You know you're unhealthy when you grow up hating yourself. Many abandoned children actually grow up hating themselves because they think the abandonment was *their fault.* They grow up having no confidence in themselves.

I often preach on grace because we are a people that have been abandoned and rejected. We have junk in our trunk. The bottom line is that we must learn how to receive healing from God and trust Him in a whole new way.

The problem is that if you do not love yourself, then you will have an even harder time truly loving anyone else.

The junk in our trunk often makes us overly sensitive to what other people say and do. Have you ever met someone who was so sensitive that you felt you had to "walk on eggshells" around them? They are so easily offended that you must guard every word you say because they might take things the wrong way.

Pain Says, "This Is Where You Need Healing"

God says lay aside the weights, even if it is painful. It helps to remember that pain is simply a confirmation sign that says, "This is the exact area where you need healing."

What does a doctor do in a physical exam? The doctor pokes and prods key areas of the body and asks, "Does that hurt? How about there? Uh oh, did that hurt? Was it a sharp jabbing pain or a dull throb?" Once the doctor finds the sore spot and confirms the suspicion, you might hear it said, "That is the area where you need attention. There is an infection in there."

The Great Physician is waiting to bind up and treat your wounds. Admit that you have junk in your trunk and stretch out your "junk," the hidden wounds and hurts in your life. It may be painful today, but God will bring you beauty for ashes and the oil of joy for mourning.

(Most people tend to dread "spring cleaning" projects and cleaning projects in general, but it is vital that we get the junk out of our trunks. Don't hesitate to contact us if you need encouragement or prayer during your "cleaning project." Visit our Internet website at www.DLministries.com).

Day 25

TURNING SHAME INTO PRAISE

And He said to him, "You shall love the Lord your God with all your heart, and with all your soul, and with all your mind." This is the great and foremost commandment. The second is like it, "You shall love your neighbor as yourself" (Mt. 22:37-39).

And they shall rebuild the old ruins, they shall raise up the former desolations, and they shall repair the ruined cities, the desolations of many generations...But you shall be named the Priests of the LORD, men shall call you the Servants of our God...*Instead of your shame you shall have double honor*, and instead of confusion they shall rejoice in their portion. Therefore in their land they shall possess double; everlasting joy shall be theirs (Isa. 61:4, 6-7; emphasis mine).

"Behold, at that time I will deal with all who afflict you; I will save the lame, and gather those who were driven

out; *I will appoint them for praise and fame* in every
land where they were *put to shame* (Zeph. 3:20).

Did you know that you can be saved and on your way to Heaven
but do something so stupid that you bring dishonor and disgrace
into your life? Few of us understand the difference between shame
and guilt, but one of them can ruin your life.

When you *do* something bad, you experience *guilt*. We all wrestle with guilt from time to time. In the world, if you are *guilty* then
you pay your fine or serve your time and hope you don't get caught
again. In Christ, you honestly repent, are forgiven, and go your
merry way with a clean heart.

The Cure for Shame: New Creature, New Life, New Identity

The Holy Spirit sometimes speaks the language of guilt to convict
us of sin, saying, "You are guilty" (see Jn. 16:8). The sole purpose of
guilt or conviction by the Holy Spirit is to lead us to repentance and
complete restoration to God.

- We feel guilty because of *the things we have done.*

- We feel shame for *what we have become.*

Shame is the language of the enemy. He says over and over, day
after day, "You are nobody, you are unworthy, your life isn't worth living. Everything about you is unacceptable and you will always be
unacceptable." The purpose of shame is to demean, dominate, and
destroy someone.

What do you see when you look in the mirror? Your spiritual enemy
wants to make you think you are a loser so he can steal your future. Has
someone from your past tried to convince you that you are no good?

Don't get angry with them, simply forgive them and totally reject
the things they said. If they said you were stupid—they were wrong.
If they said you were no good—they were wrong. If they said you
were "just like your father"—they were wrong, unless your father was
transformed through Jesus Christ into a new creature.

Turning Shame Into Praise

No Amount of Encouragement Seems to Affect Shame

Sometimes well-meaning parents make mistakes while raising their children, and they actually bring shame into a child's life. Once shame has been introduced, no amount of encouragement will seem to affect them. They simply can't believe what you are saying. It is like applying a bandage to cancer.

When shame rules someone's life, they may wish that they were never born and probably desire to die. Shame says, "You are no good. You do not deserve God's love and forgiveness." God says, "*No one* deserves My love and forgiveness, and no one is worthy; but I give it to you freely."

Shame says, "You are unworthy because of what you are." But grace says, "You are accepted and loved no matter what you are or what you have done—because of who God is."

Most people feel shame because they don't like themselves. But God's grace says, "I love you no matter what."

I believe that the healing of shame starts by understanding God's grace and His unconditional love. If you will understand that God loves you in spite of yourself, then you can understand He loves you no matter what you've done.

If someone has abused or misused you in the past and brought shame into your life, God says, "Forgive them, and *I will turn your shame into praise.*" He will take what the enemy has used as a tool to destroy your life and turn it around for your good. (He will also restore the years that have been stolen.)

It Is Not Because of You, It Is Because of Him

If you know who you are in Christ, then you know you were created in His image. You need to know that you have been adopted into the Family of God. It is not because of you, it is because of Him.

God's love for you has nothing to do with your performance. It has to do with the obedience and love of Jesus Christ. You may still feel like a loser, look like a loser, and act like a loser at times, but this Bible promise is for you: "*You are from God, little children, and have overcome them; because greater is He who is in you than he who is in the world"* (1 John 4:4).

God changes you from the inside out! Do you know who you are in Christ? Let me show you your adoption papers: "Now that you are born-again you have the spirit of adoption, and you are a joint-heir with Jesus Christ" (compiled from Rom. 8:14-17). Whatever belongs to Him belongs to you. It is not because you deserve it; it is because of the Family into which you have been adopted.

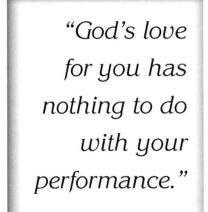

"God's love for you has nothing to do with your performance."

If you do *not* know who you are in Christ, then people will tell you that you are no good, and you will believe them. If you have *not* experienced the unconditional love of Christ in your heart, then you will believe that no one could love somebody like you.

The Hardest People to Love

You are the perfect candidate for shame if you are the kind of person who constantly needs the approval of others. That is why you must know who you are in Christ. Shame-based people usually don't like themselves. In their minds they are no good, so why should anybody else like them? The hardest people to love are people who don't like themselves.

If you don't know who you are in Christ, you will always be searching for something or someone to make you feel good about yourself. That is often the root behind addictions to sexual sins, alcoholism, and drugs.

God's Word tells us how we can begin to love ourselves. He says, you must start by loving God with all of your heart. Once you love God with all your heart, then you are free to love your fellowman. Once you love God and your fellowman, then you are free to love yourself.

You cannot live your life trying to please others. Quit living as a people-pleaser. Learn to live as God-pleaser. It doesn't matter who is on your side or who is against you, *as long as God is on your side.* "If God be for us, who can be against us?" (Rom. 8:31b, KJV)

Turning Shame Into Praise

So, you give your life to the Lord Jesus Christ. Old things pass away, behold all things become new. All your past has been washed away by the precious Blood of Jesus Christ.

Once you know who you are in Christ, you won't have to try so hard to impress people. Once you know who you are in Christ, you won't let other people's opinions of you hold you back. Once you know who you are in Christ, you can quit being like someone else and be yourself.

Your Enemy Wants to Lock You Into Your Shame

Meanwhile, understand that your spiritual enemy will be doing everything he can to lock you into your shame. Then he could keep you from living out God's plan for your life. He hopes that if you feel enough shame, then you will probably backslide and quit serving the Lord.

Shame is a normal reaction in situations involving rape, incest, divorce, domestic violence, bankruptcy, teenage pregnancy, adultery, and more.

Never forget that the devil is the accuser of the brethren. His great hope is to leverage your guilt into full-blown shame. Just remember that the church of Jesus Christ is full of people who have failed dramatically but were saved even more dramatically by the all-powerful love of Jesus.

God's heart goes out to people who sin and bring shame into their lives. In fact, He feels so much compassion for them that He says, "I will give you a double portion of joy," if you will turn to Him.

He says, "He will bind up your wounds and heal your broken heart." He says, "He will give you beauty for ashes, the oil of joy for mourning, and the garment of praise, instead of a spirit of heaviness."

He says, "I know that you have been humiliated. I know you feel rejection. I know you feel shame because of the things that have happened in your life. But I am going to give you a double portion of My joy because you trust in Me."

He says, "I know you were molested as a child. But forgive the molester, and I will turn your shame into praise." He says, "I know your husband abused you. But if you will forgive him, I will turn your shame into praise."

No matter who you are or what you've done, *you can start over today*. The Good News of Jesus Christ is all about new beginnings. Jesus died in your place to take away your shame and turn it into praise! He makes you a new person with a new beginning.

If you truly know who you are in Christ, you can be free of shame forever.

(We are dedicated to your success in Christ. If the weight of shame seems too difficult to overcome, please contact us for prayer and more extensive support. Visit our Internet website at www.DLministries.com).

Day 26

DON'T LOSE YOUR ENTHUSIASM

⚭⚭

You just don't feel it like you used to feel it. You have known the Lord for a long time, and now the thrill is gone.

You took it for granted that it would always be the way it was right after you gave your life to Jesus. God did such a supernatural miracle in your life! You were so enthusiastic that you witnessed to everything that moved—you even witnessed to the neighbor's poodle a couple of times!

What happened? You *knew* that God was real in those days. Before you surrendered to Christ, the whole church thing seemed like foolishness to you. Once Jesus came into your life, you knew that you were a different person.

You became enthusiastic about everything connected to the Lord (*enthusiasm* means "to be inspired by God"[1]). You wanted to serve in the church, you shouted all the time, and you ran more laps in church than you did at the gym! You were enthusiastic in the extreme.

Despite the best efforts of the preacher to resurrect that old excitement, you just don't feel it like you used to feel it. The music minister urges you to praise and worship God, and at special moments he even urges you to dance like you used to do...but you just stare at him with glazed-over eyes like a deer staring blankly into headlights.

Take heart, there is hope for you. Begin with the basics outlined by King David: "Enter His gates with thanksgiving, and His courts with praise." (Ps. 100:4).

Go in *with thanksgiving* if you want to see God. Some folk are so busy complaining and murmuring that they never see Him. When God sees your thanksgiving and praise, and your enthusiasm over Jesus, there is no limit to what He will do for you in your life!

Before many of us gave our hearts to the Lord, even the slightest excuse would send us flocking to the bars and nightclubs to celebrate. We would celebrate Groundhog Day with enthusiasm; singing, dancing, and making fools out of ourselves for nothing! Now that we are saved, we have to come to church and act dignified. Something is wrong with this picture.

He Is Looking For God-Pleasers, Not People-Pleasers

Our problem is that we care too much about what people think about us. The Lord is looking for someone who will get excited about Him. He is looking for God-pleasers, not people-pleasers. Quit living your life for people—one day they love you and the next they won't even take your phone call.

Some people think that we are too emotional when it comes to our praise, but they just don't know what the Bible says.

When you've been through hell and high water, you stop caring about what people think. When you've lost everything you have and then God begins to bring it back, you don't care what people think. You can be conservative if you want, but when you need a breakthrough in your life you have to quit caring about what people think of you.

Your spiritual enemy doesn't want you to get excited about the things of God. He is happiest when you are timid, faithless, or a complete captive under his influence. God, on the other hand, wants you to leave that wilderness behind and possess the land of His promises and blessings.

178

Don't Lose Your Enthusiasm

(That is not just "spiritual" territory. God wants you to own your own house and acquire property as a landowner.)

David was a little shepherd boy who was forgotten and overlooked as he tended sheep out in the fields. But God noticed his enthusiasm. Young David's thankful heart and overflowing praise caused God to promote him above his brothers. If you want to capture God's attention, you need to get exuberant and enthusiastic in your love for God. David sinned and made mistakes, but he knew how to bless and praise God, and the Lord moved on his behalf. Even though you have failed in the past, failure is never the end when you serve God.

> *"Your enthusiasm for the Lord will cause God Himself to notice you."*

Perhaps you feel no one remembers you or has noticed your talents and potential. Your enthusiasm for the Lord will cause God Himself to notice you. Maybe you have been completely overlooked because of your age, skin color, gender, or because you "don't know anyone important or powerful." Your enthusiasm for the Lord will cause God to move you to the front of the line.

Quit Saying It Is Not Your Personality and Get Excited!

If you don't have what you would call an exuberant personality, you should know there is something about enthusiasm that captures God's attention. Quit saying it is not your personality and get excited about the things of God.

God said of David, "This is a man after My own heart" (see Acts 13:22b). If you want God to be blessed, then come to church prepared to *be that blessing!* If you want to bless God, then get excited about loving Him and telling Him how wonderful He is.

David played anointed music on his harp before King Saul and the demons running Saul's life had to leave. Visitors you bring to church may find it hard to sit still when anointed music begins to play. They get uncomfortable, irritated, and can't figure out why. Anointed music stirs up demons and sets captives free. It will give you a shout and a good hallelujah.

How could little David defeat this huge giant and he just had a sling-shot. It wasn't much. The sheer power of *praise* helped little David defeat Goliath, the 9-½ foot tall professional soldier (now *that* was a giant).

You think you don't have much but you can defeat the giants in your life too. David had praise in his heart that far exceeded his brothers. When there is praise in your heart and mouth, you don't need much to defeat depression or difficulty.

The Loud One Was the One Who Received His Miracle

Blind Bartimaeus needed a miracle, and when he heard that Jesus was coming his way, the blind beggar began to cry out, "Jesus, Son of David, have mercy on me!" He was so loud, so desperate, so excited, and so enthusiastic, that everybody nearby told him to shut up. It only made him shout louder! He was the one Jesus stopped to talk to that day, and Bartimaeus—the loud one—was the person who received his miracle in that town! (See Mk. 10:46-52.)

Passionless people will line up to tell you to shut up, but God stops to work miracles for people who refuse to stop praising Him! Sometimes you have to say, "Wait a minute. You can't help me anyway! But God is passing by, and I am only a shout away from His healing, delivering, resurrecting power! Excuse me, I've got some praise to shout His way!"

People who never have problems can't understand why we praise the Lord with tears running down our faces and shout until we lose our voices. But if God has ever met you at the end of your strength and rescued you, then you understand.

I challenge you to stop saying, "It's not my personality," and begin to shout unto God with a voice of triumph! You will learn to give praise to the Lord in a new way the day your back is against the wall and trouble stares you in the face!

Don't Lose Your Enthusiasm

Wilma Rudolph had polio in both legs as a child. She wore braces but she had a dream of walking. Do you have a dream in your life? Wilma had a dream and she used her faith in the Lord to overcome her obstacles. She somehow made the basketball team in high school, and went on in aggressive faith to eventually win three gold medals for our country!

Get Aggressive and Believe the Promises

You cannot be passive if you want to see your miracle come to pass. Get aggressive and believe the promises of God. Elijah lived in a land filled with false prophets, idolaters, and psychics. He was surrounded by doubt and unbelief but he remained enthusiastic about his faith in God.

He challenged all of the false prophets to meet him for a showdown on top of Mt. Carmel. Elijah was so enthusiastic about his faith in the Lord that when he prayed, God sent fire from heaven that consumed the sacrifice, the water, the wood, and even the stones of the altar!

When God sees you prepare Him a sacrifice of enthusiastic thanksgiving, praise, and worship mixed with faith, He will send a fire into your life. It will burn away every trace of apathy, unbelief, and lukewarm religion in your soul! If you will be enthusiastic in your faith and learn to offer the sacrifice of praise to God, then He has a fire that will burn up every difficult obstacle and hard place in your life.

If you remain enthusiastic in your prayer and praise life, God's anointing will send a fire that will clear out your enemies. The enemy may come at you one way, but God will cause that enemy to run in terror *seven* ways!

Persistence defeats resistance. When you encounter all kinds of resistance in your finances, be persistent in your giving and it will cause the enemy to be defeated. Persistence in praise and worship will remove the resistance hindering your marriage and your ministry. Persistence will defeat resistance!

His Enthusiastic Courage Brought God On the Scene

Shammah was one of David's three mighty men. He won fame throughout Israel when he took his stand in the middle of a field of lentils and defended it against an entire troop of Philistine soldiers. Shammah killed the Philistine invaders and set an example of enthusiastic courage that brought God on the scene. The Bible specifically says "and the Lord brought about a great victory"! (see 2 Sam. 23:12).

You are armed with the double-edged sword called the Word of God. Take your stand in the middle of your life, marriage, family, and ministry. Praise Him and let Him bring about a great victory.

> *"Take your stand in the middle of your life, marriage, family, and ministry."*

Generations later, King Joash of Israel went to Elisha in the last days of the prophet's life. Elisha told the king to shoot an arrow through a window facing the east. Then he said it was the Lord's arrow of victory over Aram, an enemy situated in the east.

This is a prophetic picture teaching us to shoot the Lord's arrow of victory towards our enemies. Whenever you face an obstacle or problem greater than you are, take the Lord's arrow of victory—God's Word—and shoot it at your enemy.

The arrow we shoot today is the Word of God, the arrow in our mouths. (It is also the Sword of the Lord in our hands.)

The prophet's direction for King Joash wasn't complete yet. After the king shot the single arrow through the eastern window, Elisha asked him to pick up the remaining arrows and strike the ground. At this point, the king's enthusiasm seemed to grow weaker. Perhaps he looked around and felt foolish hitting the ground with a bunch of arrows.

Where Is Your Enthusiasm?

For whatever reason, the king only struck the ground three times. Then the aged man of God grew angry and essentially said, "Where is your enthusiasm?" The king should have struck the ground five or six times, and then he would have completely *destroyed* Israel's enemy. Now he would only whip Aram halfway!

God wanted King Joash to be enthusiastic about the fact that God was going to deliver him from his enemies. Lukewarm faith only gets lukewarm results, if that much!

Get enthusiastic about God! He is about to deliver you. Get excited because He is about to heal and deliver you! Praise Him with exuberance because God is about to turn your situation around!

God is looking for people who will praise Him no matter what they are going through. He is searching for somebody who will shout to Him, even when it looks as if all is lost. He is looking for men and women of *faith!*

"The kingdom of heaven suffers violence, and violent men take it by force" (Mt. 11:12b). "Blessed be the Lord, my rock, who trains my hands for war, and my fingers for battle" (Ps. 144:1).

After three hostile armies challenged Judah's King Jehoshaphat, the king called a prayer meeting and God gave him a prophetic promise of victory. In response, the king launched the battle by sending out his "praise team" ahead of his troops. This is a battle plan that *always works*:

> And when they began singing and praising, the Lord set ambushes against the sons of Ammon, Moab, and Mount Seir, who had come against Judah; so they were routed (2 Chr. 20:22).

Before you go into battle, let praise fight on your behalf! The Lord is looking for people who will be enthusiastic in their praise toward Him while trusting Him to defeat their enemies.

God has placed His arrows of victory in your hand and in your heart. Failure is not the end. It only marks the beginning of your deliverance in praise. Shoot His Word, the arrows of God, toward your enemies and challenges with enthusiasm. Stand still and see the hand of God deliver you.

> O magnify the Lord with me, and let us exalt His name together (Ps. 34:3).

(Keep your enthusiasm high for God and His kingdom. Don't hesitate to contact us for prayer or to share a testimony of God's goodness. Visit our Internet website at www.DLministries.com).

Endnotes

1. *Merriam Webster's Collegiate Dictionary, Tenth Edition* (Springfield, MA: Merriam-Webster, Incorporated, 1994), p. 386, "enthusiasm." My definition was derived from the original etymology or root words. The first dictionary definition offered was "belief in special revelations of the Holy Spirit."

Day 27

TURNING WALLS INTO BRIDGES

"The Spirit of the Lord God is upon Me, because the LORD has anointed Me to preach good tidings to the poor; He has sent Me to heal the brokenhearted, to proclaim liberty to the captives, and the opening of the prison to those who are bound; to proclaim the acceptable year of the LORD, and the day of vengeance of our God; to comfort all who mourn, to console those who mourn in Zion, to give them beauty for ashes, the oil of joy for mourning, the garment of praise for the spirit of heaviness; that they may be called trees of righteousness, the planting of the LORD, that He may be glorified. Instead of your shame you shall have double honor, and instead of confusion they shall rejoice in their portion. Therefore in their land they shall possess double; everlasting joy shall be theirs (Isa. 61:1-3, 7).

Therefore, if anyone is in Christ, he is a new creation; old things have passed away; behold, all things have

become new. Now all things are of God, who has reconciled us to Himself through Jesus Christ, and has
given us the ministry of reconciliation, that is, that
God was in Christ reconciling the world to Himself,
not imputing their trespasses to them, and has committed to us the word of reconciliation. Therefore we
are ambassadors for Christ, as though God were
pleading through us: we implore you on Christ's
behalf, be reconciled to God (2 Cor. 5:17-20).

The freedoms we enjoy in our modern society are wonderful, but
the enemy of our souls has also produced an abusive world
wracked by much heartache and pain right in the middle of outward
prosperity. Abuse seems to dominate our news—sexual abuse, physical abuse, mental abuse, and even spiritual abuse.

Any group of people will probably include many individuals
scarred by broken relationships, divorce, divorced parents, abuse,
rape, abandonment, ridicule by peers, and rejection from childhood.

Constructing Secret Walls Around Weaknesses and Insecurities

Even one of these things can leave us hurting and wounded, and
lead us to build walls of protection we described earlier. Born-again
Christians and unsaved people alike sometimes construct these
secret walls around their weaknesses and insecurities as a means of
protection.

When we prefer not to reveal our hurts to other people, we build
walls. We seem to feel they help us to cope with the unfairness experienced in the past.

The problem with walls is that they can "backfire" and produce
a *lifetime* of isolation, loneliness, and heartache. What we meant for
protection can even become our own private prison unseen by the
naked eye.

Sadly, our human ability to adapt sometimes allow us to feel this
kind of self-enforced isolation is actually "normal." In contrast, God has
made it clear in His Word that it is *not* normal for humans to be alone.

Turning Walls Into Bridges

When our walls are up, we often develop attitudes of self-pity expressed as "you owe me," "nobody will ever control me or hurt me again," or "I can't believe they treated me like that!"

God wants to bring down the walls in your life and help you replace them with bridges.

If you were raised by people who criticized everything you did, they unwittingly participated in the enemy's plan to separate you from the love of God at an early age and cause you to hate yourself.

If you were ridiculed or picked on by childhood playmates over some aspect of your physical appearance, the enemy was at work laying a subtle trap for you at a tender age.

The fruit of his dark labor is that many people today hate their noses, their chins, their legs, and their hair (or the lack thereof). They

> *"God wants to bring down the walls in your life and help you replace them with bridges."*

have fallen into the enemy's grand plan to plant self-hatred in an entire generation of people in a self-centered age. The end result is that you will reject yourself!

The Enemy Is Against You Because He Hates You

God says, " Love your neighbor *as yourself.*" Understand that the enemy is against you *because he hates you.*

God made you absolutely and totally unique, just as He makes each snowflake unique unto itself. We are different because we are supposed to be different! If two of us are exactly the same, then one of us isn't necessary.

Quit trying to be like others and be the best you can possibly be. Understand that your greatest critics in life will probably be people who really don't like themselves!

There are saved people who are on their way to Heaven, but who are surrounded by walls and merely exist from day to day in defeat with no peace, no joy, no self-control, and no love.

Overly harsh fathers may help foster attitudes of hatred in sons and daughters towards anyone in authority. Harsh mothers sometimes produce attitudes of hatred towards women in their children.

If you have a difficult time maintaining lasting relationships, then there is a very good chance that hidden walls need to be torn down in your life and replaced with godly bridges to heal others.

Any root of rejection in your life from feelings of abandonment in childhood may make it difficult for you to maintain deep and lasting relationships.

If you are battling deep feelings of anger and bitterness right now, it is a sign that you are concealing and protecting your pain.

It Is Time For a Great Jailbreak

We all seem to be involved in a great cover-up, and many of us admit that we feel as if we have been imprisoned in our own lives— *it is time for a great jailbreak right now!*

People hurt people. Even church folks have a way of saying and doing things that can hurt us at times. We think that no one can hurt us if we throw up walls of protection. However, when we throw up walls to keep others out, we eventually isolate ourselves and wall *ourselves* in!

People let you down, biting words wounded you, cruel rejection scarred you, but in the face of it all Jesus came to give you beauty for ashes! He came to tear down the walls of separation in your life. He came to help you build a bridge across the troubled waters in your life!

He is the solution to every hurt, every wound, every insecurity, every tender place of weakness, and every scarred memory of betrayal or abuse. Jesus the Bridge Builder can heal every wound and put your life back together. If something is still missing, He is able to speak into existence that which is not.

When Jesus came to this earth, He came as the Living Way, eternity's Bridge to God and His eternal kingdom. He sacrificed

Himself so that we could once again have a relationship with God the Father.

The truth is, God hates dividing walls and things that separate Him from His children. He wants to turn all of your walls into bridges. He isn't content merely to heal you of your hurts. His plan is to turn around every difficult or painful thing you have endured *so that you may help others build bridges* and tear down the walls in their lives.

Be An Instrument of Healing Toward Others

My Lord wants to give you beauty for ashes and turn your scars into stars. He wants to bind up your wounds, so that you can be an instrument of healing toward others. After He has healed you of your brokenness, He expects you to be His vehicle to heal others. He wants to help you build bridges so you can help others.

The Lord has called you to be a vehicle to carry others across the Bridge of Jesus Christ. This is what Paul the apostle called "the ministry of reconciliation" given to us as Christ's ambassadors:

> Now all these things are from God, who reconciled us to Himself through Christ, and *gave us the ministry of reconciliation*, namely, that God was in Christ reconciling the world to Himself, not counting their trespasses against them, and *He has committed to us the word of reconciliation*. Therefore, we are ambassadors for Christ, as though God were entreating through us; we beg you on behalf of Christ, be reconciled to God (2 Cor. 5:18-20).

Forgiveness is a gift given to people who don't deserve it. You and I didn't deserve to be forgiven, but now we must forgive others who don't deserve to be forgiven either. Unforgiveness is a poison that causes you to be bitter. God wants to take the bitterness and poison out of you right now.

God created you for love and not hate. You were designed and born to be an instrument of forgiveness, not an instrument of rejection. Cross the bridge of Christ and tear the walls down today.

Passing Through Doorways of Pain to Get Healed

Emotional healing can be painful, and sometimes we have to pass through doorways of pain to get healed. It is time to stop hiding your pain.

We have been taught that we need to believe in ourselves, but I openly admit that apart from the Lord Jesus Christ, I am nothing.

We don't need self-confidence; we need confidence in the Lord Jesus Christ. The next time the enemy says you are nothing but a failure, answer him: "That is right. But the Greater One in me is not a failure, and I am more than a conqueror through Christ Jesus."

I have finally learned that He is my Strength, my Shield, and He is the Conqueror. I am just along for the ride. He is my Confidence, my Peace, and my Joy. He is the Vine.

Yes, people have let you down and they have hurt you. Now is the time to bring down the walls and begin to build (and cross) some bridges. It is time to get your past behind you and bring those walls down (Rev. 12:11).

You may sow in tears, but you will reap in joy and singing. Weeping may endure for the night, but joy comes in the morning. Yes, I can handle the pain today, as long as I know my healing is coming tomorrow.

Jesus came to set you free and bring full release from every form of bondage. He came to give you beauty for ashes.

Whatever you have gone through in your life; let nothing steal your future! God wants you to live before you die. He wants you to enjoy life, and He wants you to tear the walls down and build bridges.

All you have to do today is confess your sins, admit your heartaches and point out your pains to the Lord. All you have to do is admit to the Lord the prison of pain that you have been in and He will heal you.

It's time to shift the focus from your problems to the Problem Solver. He's the Lover of your soul, your divine Bridge over troubled waters. Now is the time to tear down every wall in your life and turn them into bridges!

(Sometimes we need prayer support and godly assistance to bring down the walls in our lives. We are here to help you. Don't hesitate to contact us through our Internet website at www.DLministries.com).

Day 28

WHEN YOU'VE LOST EVERYTHING

"The Spirit of the Lord God is upon Me, because the LORD has anointed Me to preach good tidings to the poor; He has sent Me to heal the brokenhearted, to proclaim liberty to the captives, and the opening of the prison to those who are bound; to proclaim the acceptable year of the LORD, and the day of vengeance of our God; to comfort all who mourn, to console those who mourn in Zion, to give them beauty for ashes, the oil of joy for mourning, the garment of praise for the spirit of heaviness; that they may be called trees of righteousness, the planting of the LORD, that He may be glorified (Isa. 61:1-3).

Y̲ou and I have a spiritual enemy who aligns himself squarely against us. His pure purpose is to execute a death sentence on your life in some way. He isn't picky. He will be happy to do it through divorce, or a cheating spouse, the death of a child, or the death of a God-given dream.

He intends to leave such a trail of brokenness and shattered dreams in your life that you begin to believe you can never recover from the encounter. He won't be content until your life is in a thousand pieces or totally destroyed.

> *"Consider the source... your enemy is a liar."*

The problem with most people is that they reach such a point of discouragement that they don't want to go to a pastor, a counselor, or even to a church service. It is all part of the enemy's plan to separate and isolate you from what and Whom you need the most.

Consider the source...your enemy is a liar. God has a plan for your life—a good one. You may feel like Humpty-Dumpty, looking at your shattered life scattered in a thousand pieces. My God is ready and waiting to put you back together again and bring wholeness into your life!

Millions of people have come to a place where they feel they have lost everything. It happens for various reasons including disobedience, stubbornness, plain old rebellious human nature, difficult circumstances beyond their control, or even the outright attack of the enemy.

We all experience brokenness from time to time, and pain is no respecter of persons. If your life is broken today for any of these reasons, you need to know that God does His best work in times of brokenness.

God Loves You Unconditionally

The Bible says, "The Lord is near to the brokenhearted, and saves those who are crushed in spirit" (Ps. 34:18). God understands where you are and how you feel—even if *you* have caused all the trouble in your life! He loves you unconditionally and He hasn't forgotten about you. He has not "kicked you to the curb."

Our magnificent God has a way of turning around the worst of situations and using them for our good. He even uses the brokenness

192

of our lives to lift us higher in His purposes than we have ever been. The Bible says, "And we know that God causes all things to work together for good to those who love God, to those who are called according to His purpose" (Rom. 8:28).

No matter what mistakes you've made in your life, understand that God will never turn you away. Aren't you glad that God isn't mad at you? Religion is mad and people are mad, but God is not.

If you have made some big mistakes in your life, you may wonder if God can ever use you. The Lord never leaves people in their failures if they seek Him. He is the God of grace and mercy who restores lost things and lifts up the fallen. He will help you even when you have messed up. Remember, this is the Father who so loved the sinful world that He sent His own Son to save it (see Jn. 3:16).

My God Specializes In Impossible Situations

I don't know what happened to leave you with nothing but ashes, but I *do* know that my God specializes in turning impossible situations around! It is His delight to take ugly and painful situations and making something beautiful out of them.

If you feel your life has been reduced to nothing but ashes, you need to know that God loves you and He is attracted to you. He is ready to heal your brokenness and revive your crushed spirit. He will lift you up if you cannot lift yourself, *but* you must call Him or come after Him.

Even though He loves you, God cannot bless you until you come into obedience to His Word. His love is free and unconditional; but he can only help you after you seek His face.

God doesn't have time or mercy for the proud or self-sufficient. He loves sinner and saint alike, but God knows the proud will fall in due time because they've built their lives on sand. If you will *humble yourself*, He will move heaven and earth on your behalf!

Pray this prayer with me if you see yourself in this place of brokenness and ashes: "God, I messed up. I thought I was going the right way. I thought I was doing the right thing. I messed up. I need Your forgiveness. I need Your help. Jesus, forgive me and come into my life." Now go after God and watch what He will do.

It doesn't matter that you feel you are in your midnight hour—it isn't too late! God always does His best work at midnight.

It was midnight when Paul and Silas were in prison early in the life of the church. Their situation seemed hopeless, but they began to praise God in that prison! We have a lot to learn from Paul and Silas. They began to praise Him and worship Him in the midst of their nightmare and God literally shook that jail cell until those men were miraculously set free!

He Is At His Best When You Come To the End of Yourself!

I have discovered that God does His best work when people come to the end of themselves and are broken and crushed. Perhaps that is because when we finally stop depending on ourselves, we begin to lean on God.

God's power is revealed in our weakness. He is at His best when we stand in the failures of our past and say, "God, I give it to You."

God uses the weak things of this world to confound the wise (see 1 Cor. 1:27). If your toes are covered in the ashes of your dreams and failures, you are a prime candidate for a miracle! God uses people that you and I would *never* use! I would have never used David, or Peter or Moses. They were all two and three-time losers. (I *know* I would have never used a guy like Dennis Leonard!)

If your resume reads "broken" and "covered in ashes," then you are at the right place at exactly the right time. It is when you've got nothing to offer except yourself that God will give you beauty for ashes.

If you feel discouraged because of the unfairness of your situation, God says, "Give Me your ashes, I will make something beautiful out of them."

In the original Hebrew scriptures, the fire of God fell from heaven and consumed the burnt sacrifice. Everything on the altar was consumed, leaving nothing behind but ashes.

God commanded the priest to save the ashes after the special offering of the red heifer was consumed. Ashes are what is left over after a fire. They really don't look like much. That is the way the ashes of your life's dreams look after the crisis passes. Praise God, little becomes much in the hands of the Lord.

When You've Lost Everything

Ashes are what you have left when you've gone through hell in your life and you have nowhere to turn. You feel you only have a pile of ashes after you go through a divorce or the breakup of a relationship. Give Him the ashes that are left over after someone says to you, "I don't love you any more."

Give God a Little Bit and He Will Make a Miracle of It

My God is so big that if you just give him a little bit, He will make a miracle out of it. Give Him the ashes of your life and trust Him to do something great in your life.

It is time for somebody to tell you the truth as God sees it: the enemy is lying to you! God loves you, and He has a plan and a purpose for your life.

"If you're standing in nothing but ashes today, just know that God is about to turn it around!"

When you have nothing left but ashes, that is the best place you can be. That is when you can say, "Lord, I give up." When you come to the end of yourself, that's when God can give you beauty for ashes.

You may think that you are so far down that God can't help you. You may feel like such a failure because all of the ashes that are in your life. But you don't need much to see God help you. All you need are just some ashes.

It may not seem like much to you, but a little becomes a lot in God's hands. A few fish, a little bit of bread becomes a lot in God's hands. God will take what the enemy meant to destroy you and He'll turn it for your good. When you've lost everything you're in a place for God to move in your life.

You Are Standing In Ashes, But God Is About to Turn It Around!

If you're standing in nothing but ashes today, just know that God is about to turn it around! No weapon formed against you shall prosper.

God made me to be the head and not the tail. He made me to be blessed coming in and blessed going out. He made me and everything that I touch would be blessed.

You may be standing in nothing but ashes today, but "many are the afflictions or troubles of the righteous, but the Lord shall deliver them out of them all. Surely goodness and mercy shall follow you all the days of your life and you shall dwell in the house of the Lord."

God is going to use all of your trouble for your good. He's even going to use it to change your life.

You may have a lot of pain today, but the pain is going to make you a better person. The pain is going to make you more loving. The pain is going to make you more understanding. The pain is going to make you more forgiving. And the pain is going to make you more like Jesus.

Even if you feel your marriage has been reduced to ashes, this is your year for a breakthrough. "This is my year for a breakthrough. This is my year for a business breakthrough! This is my year for a ministry breakthrough! This is my year!"

The Bible promises us, "Weeping may last for the night, but a shout of joy comes in the morning" (Ps. 30:5b). Dawn is coming, your weeping is over; and I can hear a shout rising up in your heart! God says, "I know you've gone through hell and high water, but this is a new day when I am doing a new thing in your life."

Failure, brokenness, and shattered dreams are not the end for you. I declare that you were *born for such a time as this*. I can tell you that God picked me up and turned *me* around. He gave me beauty for ashes, and I know He doesn't show preferences. *God will do the same thing for you!*

(God seems to be especially careful to answer the cries of the brokenhearted. If you feel as if you have lost everything, we are dedicated to see you step into God's total provision and supply. Don't hesitate to contact us through our Internet website at www.DLministries.com).

Day 29

I'M CLAIMING MY INHERITANCE

For you have not received a spirit of slavery [or a spirit of bondage] leading to fear again. But you have received a spirit of adoption, as sons, by which we cry out Abba Father. The spirit himself bears witness with our spirit that we are children of God and *if children then also heirs of God and fellow heirs with Christ.* If indeed we suffer with Him that we may also be glorified with Him (Rom. 8:15-17).

...in order that in Christ Jesus the blessing of Abraham might come to the Gentiles, so that we might receive the promise of the Spirit through faith...And *if you belong to Christ,* then *you are Abraham's offspring, heirs according to promise* (Gal. 3:14, 29).

What do you do when it is time to receive an inheritance? *You consult the will.* Then you *execute the will.*

In our case, we must pull out the original will given to Abraham many generations before Joshua actually led the descendents of

Abraham, Isaac, and Jacob into the Promised Land. God deeded to Abraham and his physical and spiritual descendants by faith:

> ...great and splendid cities which you did not build, and houses full of all good things which you did not fill, and hewn cisterns which you did not dig, vineyards and olive trees which you did not plant, and you shall eat and be satisfied" (Deut. 6:10b-11).

God said, "I will bless those that love me for a thousand generations." Our problem is that most of the folks in the Family of God don't even know who they are. You have to know who you are and shed the wilderness mentality if you want to possess your inheritance.

Once you discover that you are a son and joint heir, you will quit acting like a slave. God can do more for me in five minutes than I can do for myself in a lifetime.

You have to know you are a son to claim what is rightfully yours. In the original Hebrew Scriptures, the firstborn son was the rightful heir of the family inheritance, and he received a double portion of the family inheritance, as compared to the other children.

So What Are We Waiting For?

In the Renewed Covenant, God calls *all* of us (male and female) sons of inheritance. So what are we waiting for? It is time to possess the land God promised us as sons and joint heirs with Jesus. It is time *right now* to go after the things God says we can have!

- Go after your healing, because God says it is yours.

- Go after your property, because God says it's yours.

- Go after a good family and a good relationship, because God says it's yours.

- Go after the abundant life, because God says it is yours.

Daddy already left it to you, but if you don't know the inheritance is yours, then you will act like a slave. When you know who you are in Christ, then you will know that as a joint heir you are supposed to be blessed.

I'm Claiming My Inheritance

When you know that you are a son, you will have the ability of God on your life. You *know* that God will help you get a house that you know you're not qualified to get. Even though you know your failures in the past have damaged your credit rating, you know your Daddy will show you how to clean up that credit and enjoy supernatural favor with lenders.

When you know that you are a son, you know you are going to come out on top no matter what you go through today. When you are obedient and submitted to God as a son, you know that *no weapon formed against you is going to prosper!* The enemy may pull out every trick in his bag, but when you know that you are a son and a joint heir of your Daddy's inheritance, you will know that you're going to come out on top before this thing is over.

Eating From Fruit Trees You Did Not Plant

When you know you are a son, you know that you are not a grasshopper, but a royal priesthood and a holy nation. When you are a son, He will give you crops that you did not grow and you will eat from fruit trees that you did not plant.

What does that mean? That means that He'll begin to bless you in things and in ways that you don't deserve. People will give you stuff and they won't even know why they are giving it to you. People who don't even like you will help you because you are a son.

When you know you are a son, you will drink from wells that you did not dig. When you are a son, you will gain riches that you did not deserve; but it is only because you are a son of inheritance (male *or* female).

When you know you are a son, your Father will get you that house, even though you know it was more than what you deserve. When you are a son, somebody will help you get the down payment that you know you don't have. "But as it is written, Eye hath not seen, nor ear heard, neither have entered into the heart of man, the things which God hath prepared for them that love him" (1 Cor. 2:9, KJV). Since I love Him, it must mean that God has prepared a lot for me.

> In order that he might redeem those who were under
> the law that we might receive the spirit of adoption as

sons and because you are sons, God has sent forth the spirit of His son into our hearts, crying Abba Father. Therefore you are no longer a slave but a son. And if a son, then an heir through God (Gal. 4:5-7).

Now We Are Sons and No Longer Slaves

We were slaves before we gave our lives to the Lord. We were slaves to our temper, to our lusts and to our desires. We were slaves to bitterness and unforgiveness. We were slaves to our flesh. But now that we are sons, we are no longer slaves. Whether we are male or female we are sons of inheritance.

When you know you are a son, you will not do drugs, commit adultery, or cheat on your taxes. Once you know who you are in Christ, you won't be sleeping with just anybody and you will never steal God's tithe again.

When you know you are a son, you will understand that your destination is the land of God's promises. You may not know exactly how you will get there, but you are going there just the same. It doesn't matter what happened yesterday or last year. You are not looking back to the past because are now a son and joint heir with Jesus Christ. There is no longer any reason or advantage to blame other people for things you don't have. You have been given *all* things in Christ.

A slave is afraid of the future. A slave doesn't know what is going to happen to him next because he has no rights. A son, however, has hope for the future because he knows he has an inheritance. A son has a right to the family name, the Name above every name.

When you know you are a son, you cannot let fear control you. Now that you know you are the righteousness of God, you know your best days are still ahead. We know that whatever belongs to Jesus belongs to us.

You Don't Deserve the Inheritance, But It's In the Will

Do you know who you are in Christ? When you know who you are in Christ you'll stop begging God. When you know who you are in Christ, then you will know that even though you don't deserve the inheritance it's in the Will.

When you know you are a son, you can let go of the past. When you know that you're a son you can quit holding things against folk. Even though somebody gets ahead of you it don't make any difference, because you're a son of inheritance and you're going to get there too.

When you know you are a son, you know you need to be a *property owner*. You will not live in a raggedy apartment all your life. You may be living in the apartment now, but you are not staying there because you are a son of inheritance. You are the seed of Abraham, so you are supposed to be blessed. If you are broke, how can God use you to any extent? The kingdom cannot be fulfilled on this earth if God's people don't own property. Trust Him to make a way where there is no way.

When you know you are a son, you also know you are *not* a grasshopper. You have a right to walk in His blessings because you are a joint heir with Jesus Christ. You've got to know who you are in Christ and take the land with courage and authority.

> *"You have a right to walk in His blessings because you are a joint heir with Jesus Christ."*

Step Across the "Property Line" By Faith

It's time to possess the land. It's time to realize that you are the head and not the tail. It's time for you to rise up from where you are and step across the "property line" of the Jordan by faith.

It doesn't matter if people have beaten you down all your life and told you that you are no good and will never amount to anything. *You found out that you are a son, and co-heir of your Father's inheritance.*

Now it is time to claim your inheritance. If you *don't* claim it; if you don't know what is in the will, then you can't get it.

God says that if you will bring Him your tithes and offerings, He will prove Himself to you. God said, "No weapon formed against you is going to prosper." But you've got to get your attitude turned around and know who you are in Christ.

The Bible plainly teaches that poverty is a curse, so obviously it is not God's will for you or any other adopted son or daughter to be broke! You only own property when you step across that Jordan River into the Promised Land. "I'm going in. I'm not staying here. I'm getting out of this place. I'm in the wilderness today, but don't send me any UPS packages because I'm not staying here. I'm moving out of here."

God says that if we will obey Him that His blessings will overtake us. Stop apologizing for God's blessings in your life. You're supposed to be blessed. You're a son of inheritance and the seed of Abraham. God says, "I swear that I am going to bless you. I swear I'm going to bless your children. I swear I am going to prosper you, even to a thousand fold. It is your time to be blessed."

Sons Know They are Going Somewhere

Slaves don't think about tithing because they don't have anything to tithe off of. Slaves live in the wilderness anyway. But sons know they are going somewhere. Sons know they're going into their promised land. Sons know that it's only a matter of time until this thing turns around.

The Bible says that the wealth of the wicked is stored up for the righteous. I am the righteousness of God, and that means that the sinner is working to get the wealth delivered to me. Since I'm the righteousness of God, through the Blood of Jesus Christ, that means it is stored up for me.

I'm going to have to begin to use my faith. I've got to be a covenant keeper and not a covenant breaker. And all I have to do is put Him first and claim what is mine.

I'm Claiming My Inheritance

God has His blessings stored up for those who love Him. Since I love Him, I believe His blessings are in my life. You can live a life of being broke if you want to, but I plan on being blessed.

Even if you are facing a hopeless situation today, you need to hear the voice of your adopted Father say, "I love you. I'm not mad at you. I have a better life for you."

God says, "I have placed the land before you, but you've got to go possess it." God said you've got to know what your inheritance is. He said, "I left you in the will. But you've got to know what's in the will for you." Even if you have bad credit, God says, "I'll make a way where there is no way. Even if the odds are greatly against you, put Me first and I'll turn that thing around." Failure is not the end with God.

God says, "I brought you out of Egypt with a mighty hand, and I'm going to bring you out of your problems today with a mighty hand. I know you have failed in the past but I'm going to turn it for your good anyhow."

I made some mistakes in the past. I have some regrets about my past failures and actions, but that was then and this is now.

I have stayed on this mountain long enough. Now I'm going to a new place. I've been in the desert long enough. I'm going into my Promised Land.

Failure really *isn't* the end! You see, I just found out who I am in Christ! I just found out I'm a son of inheritance, and I must claim my inheritance *today*."

(We are dedicated to serving God and to blessing others in His kingdom. Don't hesitate to contact us through our Internet website at www.DLministries.com).

FAILURE IS NOT THE END

Day 30

YOU CAN'T QUIT

But you, be sober in all things, endure hardship, do the work of an evangelist, fulfill your ministry. For I am already being poured out as a drink offering, and the time of my departure has come. I have fought the good fight, I have finished the course, I have kept the faith (2 Tim. 4:5-7).

Paul the apostle wrote these words from prison, possibly the very night before he was beheaded! He laid down his life to the Lord after investing his years in preaching the Gospel.

Now at the end of his life, he was looking back at his track record. He wrote in this letter to his spiritual son, Timothy: "Endure hardship, do the work of an evangelist and fulfill your ministry."

You may think that you sit in the pews or chairs and your minister preaches the Word, visits the sick, and evangelizes the lost. The truth is that *you* are the minister, and the pastor is your drill sargeant/equipper. His job is to equip you for the ministry *because you are a full-time minister.*

You may be a postal worker, a doctor, a construction foreman, a lawyer, or a fulltime mother—but in God's eyes you became a full-time minister when you give your life to Him.

God called you to be a minister of reconciliation the moment you gave your life to Christ. His divine purpose and destiny for you goes way beyond just doing your work, eating meals, and going to bed.

> **"God wants you to have a good report..."**

There is more. The Bible says we will face hardships and persecution simply because we want to live godly lives! (see 2 Tim. 3:12) Most people are ready to leave the church if the air conditioning setting is five degrees too low or if the preacher puts too many demands on them for volunteer service—so they *really* don't like any talk of persecution. Discomfort or risk are not politically correct terms in this era of "microwave Christianity."

The fact is that once you give your life to the Lord Jesus Christ, *it is no longer about you—it is all about Him!*

Growth, challenges, difficulty, persecution; they all require faith and determination to make it through them. God wants you to have a good report—a positive declaration—in your mouth even if you are in the wilderness. God calls negative or doubting talk an evil report. When you have a good report on good days and bad days, you are demonstrated publicly that you have faith in God and His faithfulness.

What You Are Made Of

Don't say, "God, use me for Your glory," if you are not willing to witness and testify on your job! Be prepared to back up your words by enduring trouble and affliction in your life. These tests and obstacles quickly show you what you are made of, and prove whether or not you are worthy to call yourself a believer in Jesus Christ.

God honors perseverance and persistence. Dr. W.A. Criswell tells a story about his friend's two bird dogs. One day a little bulldog crawled under the fence to fight the two huge bird dogs. The little dog was thoroughly beaten and ran home.

You Can't Quit

The next day, the same thing happened. Again, the small bulldog ran home licking his wounds. After two weeks of showing up under that fence for another battle with the two bird dogs, *the little dog won* and the two dogs avoided him!

This little dog was not the strongest or the fastest, but *in his heart he was a champion*. He was the last one standing because he was too legit to quit.

You may have failed in the past, but in your heart you know you are a champion. You can't quit now—you are too close to your miracle!

Persevere leaves you still standing when all of your critics and opponents have quit. Your flesh will always want to quit when the going gets tough, but have faith in God and take your stand.

People *will* come against you if you intend to do anything for the Lord, so you must develop the tenacity to "take a lickin' and keep on tickin'." You cannot be a wimp and serve the Lord Jesus Christ.

Put On Your Spiritual Boxing Gloves

Paul said, "I have fought the good fight." Let me make it clear: *The only time a fight is good is if you win.* Discover what God says belongs to you and then put on your spiritual boxing gloves. Declare in the authority of Jesus Christ, "Devil, get your hands off my stuff!" God is looking for fighters who will fight God's way, not man's fleshly way.

Roll up your sleeves and tell the enemy that you are not going down without a fight! Make sure he knows going to have a painful and difficult fight on his hands. You know the truth, that "...No weapon that is formed against you shall prosper" (see Isa. 54:17).

And the brethren over came him – talking about the devil – by the Blood of the Lamb and the word of their testimony. So, I've got the Blood of Jesus. I speak the Blood and I testify, "Devil you can't beat me, the Blood is against you."

So Paul said, "I have finished my course." It doesn't matter how you start out, what matters is how you finish. A lot of folks start a lot of things but they don't finish. The Jordan River is full of life, but it flows into the Dead Sea where everything is dead.

It doesn't matter how you start out. What matters is how you finish up. It doesn't matter that you start out life full of joy if you end up in bitterness. What good is it?

"Start and Stop Mentality" Alert!

Our culture is developing a start and stop mentality. People don't want to finish anything they start today. They start a job and don't want to finish it. They start a business and don't want to finish. They start a marriage and don't want to finish. We should issue a "Start and Stop Mentality Alert" in the church. More and more Christians start tithing and don't want to finish. They start Bible College and don't want to finish. They start counseling and don't want to finish. They start in the choir and don't want to finish.

Judas started out with the Lord but he didn't finish with the Lord. What good is it to start out with Him and not finish with Him?

Find something that you put on hold and finish it yourself. What is it that you started off doing and you didn't finish it? You need to finish something you've started, just to prove that you can finish something.

Don't let the enemy's attacks make you a quitter. When he attacks you, the human tendency is to say, "I'm going to drop out of the choir. I'm going to drop out of the children's ministry. I'm going to drop out of the ushers department." What good is it to start something and not finish it?

When attacks, difficulties, or obstacles come, *fight the good fight of faith.* Don't quit! Failure isn't the end—it is *never* the end. It merely marks the beginning of your greatest success in Christ! The only time you are a true failure is if you quit.

God has a plan that is just for you. No one can finish that plan but you! Put your hand to the plow and *plow!* Don't look back, and don't give up. And don't look over at the next field to compare yourself with someone else! It will just cause you to get off track and make a mess. Just be the unique person God created you to be. He broke the mold when he made you.

You Can't Quit

Running a Marathon Race for Destiny

A lot of people start the Christian race, but not everyone finishes it. Most people think it is a short sprint like the 100-yard dash. No, you and I are involved in a marathon race for destiny. We are not content merely to show up, we must cross the finish line and finish the race. What good is it to start and not finish?

Compromise has become the favorite sport in God's house, and He isn't amused. People are dropping out left and right saying, "I didn't sign up for all of this hassle. This is too hard. I like to live life *my* way and on *my* terms."

Compromise is all around us, but God has called us to finish what we have started. In this race of endurance, it doesn't matter if you finish first or last—as long as you finish. Perhaps you have failed before this, but just because you have failed doesn't mean you are a failure. The only way you can be a failure is if you refuse to get back up and get back in the race for the finish line.

The church is called to rally around each runner on God's team. A man who was running a 26-mile marathon was ready to quit at Mile 23. His daughter had come to watch her dad run, and she saw him almost quit. Immediately she jumped off the curb and began to run alongside her father, encouraging him along the way. "Come on Dad, we can make it. I know we can make it."

Perhaps you picked up this book because you are at the Mile 23 marker and wondering if you should quit. My word to you is this: If you will just keep going a little further, *you can make it!* It is just a little further."

When you are serving God, failure is never the end! Failure simply marks the turning point where you can get everything turned around in your life! Your future is ahead of you.

The honeybee is one of God's supreme models of perseverance. A single honeybee travels more than eight miles and visits 400 flowers to produce *one tablespoon* of honey! That is perseverance. We must have perseverance in our lives if we want to do what God has called us to do.

Never quit. Anytime you give up, the enemy simply moves on in to destroy you. Even if you get knocked down in life, keep going until you wear the enemy out; back him down, and send him running with his tail between his legs in Jesus' name!

Don't believe a word or whisper that comes out of the enemy's mouth. This is how you know he is lying—if his "lips" are moving. All he can *do* is lie. Don't take a single word from him.

If you have dropped out of the race, confess your failure to God and allow Him to lift you back up and move you back into the race! Get back to prayer, back to tithing, back to reading your Bible and serving God.

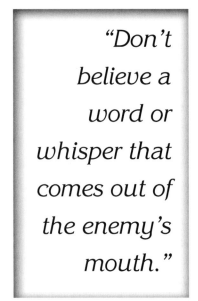

"Don't believe a word or whisper that comes out of the enemy's mouth."

I mentioned the Olympic track star, Wilma Rudolph, earlier in the book. She was the 20th of 22 children and was born prematurely. She contracted double pneumonia twice, scarlet fever, and polio in her left leg. At the age of 11, she started believing God that she would take her braces off and walk someday.

It Isn't Falling Down That Makes You a Failure

When her parents weren't home, she would take off her braces and ask God to help her walk. Some times her legs were so weak that she would fall down. But Wilma never stayed down. She always got back up. (It isn't the falling down that makes you a failure, it is the "not getting back up" that qualifies you for that.)

Wilma's high school basketball referee invited her to tryout for the Tennessee State track team. She trained hard and at the age of 16 went to the 1956 Olympics in Australia. She brought home a bronze metal in the women's 400-meter relay team. That is when she committed herself to be the best she could be at the next Olympics in 1960.

Rather than follow the path of least resistance, Wilma worked harder than anyone else on her team. She ran at 6:00 and 10:00 in the morning and at 3:00 each afternoon for about 1200 days! It was difficult and painful, but Wilma decided to persevere no matter her circumstances.

Wilma went to the 1960 Olympics in Rome and returned with three gold metals. This disadvantaged girl was the first woman in history to win three gold metals in track and field events. She was a champion because she never quit.

Before you accept defeat in your life, put your gaze back on Jesus and step back in the race! Hit your knees and pray until something happens in your family, in your finances, in your marriage, in your church.

Maybe you have failed in your life. Listen, if you will begin to trust in the Lord, then He will begin to turn things around for you! God is not mad at you (even if you deserve it).

Don't quit now. Failure is not the end. Keep the faith, and press for the mark. The Christian life is not about being perfect or doing everything right. It is about keeping the faith and finishing the course by trusting God with all of your heart.

You can overcome *all* of the failures in your life. Put God first, quit blaming others, examine yourself honestly, work on your own issues, and eventually you can overcome all of the failures of your past.

Understand the link between failure and a resistance to change. The children of Israel experienced countless failures because they wouldn't change. When fear comes your way, let the perfect love of God cast it out. Allow failure to lead you to your potential and *watch your attitude.*

Allow the Lord to change you and reprogram you from the inside out—it is the only way to break negative attitudes and take your life off of "hold." If anger shows up day after day, ask God to show you the root of your frustration and allow Him to remove it. Chances are good that you will have to forgive someone to be free, so be quick to forgive that you may be forgiven.

Remember: What happened yesterday was yesterday. That was then, this is now. You've gotta work on your anger issues. You gotta learn to forgive people. You've got to start changing in your life if you are going to overcome the failures of your past.

If the yoke around your neck has been financial, then immediately take the steps we've talked about to set yourself free. Do things God's way and enjoy His blessings. Do not fear change; embrace and welcome it. It will improve your life. Don't get down on yourself—life is a continuous process and you are coming out of the past!

Don't trust your feelings along the way, and don't feel you must control everything and everyone in your life. God is on the job and He is good at it. Settle down and enjoy the ride of your life. Allow every crisis to become a turning point toward greatness and godliness as you trust God. Pray, because prayer really does change things. As you pray, be prepared to help God get the junk out of your trunk and watch Him turn your shame into praise.

Keep your enthusiasm and stand in amazement as God transforms the walls of your life into bridges to other people and your destiny. Even if you feel you have lost everything, you serve a God who is well able to restore all. Claim your inheritance in Christ Jesus and above all—*don't quit!*

Failure is not the end. It is an opportunity for a fresh beginning in God. Make changes and start working on your stuff. Put God first in all things and trust Him. Then He will help you overcome all of the failures of your past and fulfill your eternal destiny.

(You may not feel it, and you may not see it, but you are closer than you think to victory over your failures and disappointments. Don't quit now. We are dedicated to serving you and God's kingdom in any way we can. If you would like further information, teaching, or prayer, don't hesitate to contact us through our Internet website at www.DLministries.com.)

PRAYER OF SALVATION

❧❧

God loves you...no matter who you are, no matter what your past. God loves you so much that He gave His only begotten Son for you.

The Bible tells us that *"...whoever believes in Him shall not perish but have eternal life" (John 3:16 NIV).*

Jesus laid down His life so that we could spend eternity with Him in heaven and experience His absolute best on earth. If you would like to receive Jesus Christ as your Lord and Savior, say the following prayer out loud and mean it from your heart.

Heavenly Father, I come to You admitting that I am a sinner. Right now, I choose to turn away from sin, and I ask You to cleanse me from all unrighteousness. I believe that Your Son, Jesus, died on the cross to take away my sins. I also believe that He rose again from the dead so that I might be forgiven of my sins and made righteous through faith in Him. I call upon the name of Jesus to be the Lord and Savior of my life. Jesus, I choose to follow You and ask that You fill me with the power of the Holy Spirit. I declare right now that I am a child of God. I am free from sin and full of the righteousness of God. I am saved in Jesus' name. Amen.

ALSO BY DENNIS LEONARD

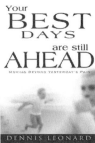

It's time to let go of past spiritual failures and make plans for a future made strong and prosperous by the power of His might. Living your life just any old way guarantees disappointment. Serve an eviction notice on the devil, and tell him you are through with that grasshopper mentality. In *Your Best Days Are Still Ahead*, Bishop Dennis Leonard invites you to turn your life around-experience a promised land-when you live your life God's way.

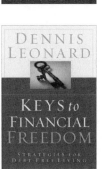

Keys to Financial Freedom

In today's unstable economic landscape, financial insecurity is the constant companion of many struggling to make ends meet. In *Keys to Financial Freedom,* Dennis Leonard offers readers a deliberate choice. Through proven, life-changing strategies, you can learn to assess your financial condition, build new money-management habits, and draw up a financial plan. Then as your wealth and prosperity grow, your faith ignites, and you experience the success of your dreams.

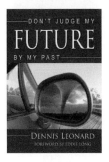

Don't Judge My Future By My Past

The Bible says that every person sins and falls short of the glory of God. But past failures can only bring guilt and condemnation. And when you live in the past, it's impossible to see a future filled with hope. In *Don't Judge My Future By My Past*, Bishop Leonard reveals God's good plan for each of us. It's a new day when you let God work in and through you.